The Little Book of Persuasion

Sia Mohajer

Table of Contents

A Short History of Persuasion

Her name was Peitho. A devoted assistant to Aphrodite—the Greek goddess of love and wisdom. To the ancient Greeks, her beauty was a reminder of her power and importance. Her legacy now only remains on a series of broken vases in an Italian museum. Her ancient Greek name was that of *Πειθώ*——meaning persuasion. In an ancient society ruled by social laws and formalities, the power of Peitho remained the one true way to achieve your ends. A man asking for a daughter's hand in marriage was required to summon the power of Peitho to be given permission. To the ancient Greeks the power of persuasion formed the basis for all successful businesses, bridal prices, marriage and politics. Bending others to your will was not a matter of just shallow consideration but rather the most fundamental pursuit. Without the power of Peitho one could not hope to carve out a place in ancient Greece.

The Greek love for persuasion formed the cornerstone of what they called rhetoric. Rhetoric is simply defined as the art of effective, persuasive speaking or writing. The politics of ancient Greece demanded that all citizens be skilled in rhetoric. The assembly where trials were held was the blueprint for the modern courtroom; it tested the effectiveness and techniques of rhetoric. Rhetoric formed the basis of classical education just as math or English would today. The ancient Greek philosopher Aristotle believed all men should learn the art of persuasion for four vital reasons.

1. Truth and justice are perfect. If you lose it is the fault of the speaker, not the situation.

2. It is the ultimate tool for teaching.

3. A good rhetorician needs to be able to argue both sides to adequately understand the entire problem and all available options.

4. It is the ultimate way to defend oneself.

The quality of a man was judged upon his ability to defend and convey his message in an eloquent manner and appeal to the hearts of those listening and speak to them so much that they would side with him. Rhetoric was an art and was treated as such. Trials were a form of public spectacle; citizens would travel to watch intellectuals engage in discussion. There was an appreciation for persuasion as an art form. Despite the logical basis for all good arguments, the ancient Greeks did not extend this to more egalitarian realms—women, slaves and inferior people were not allowed to engage in the political arena. It was a man's world, a world of privilege and power where persuasion was the ultimate weapon.

Persuasion represents something deep within man, a primal need to exert one's will over another. If ideas are our bullets, persuasion is the instrument we use to dismantle others' wills and force them on to our side. It may be a weapon but it is one that comes wearing the disguise of art. The art of storytelling is the most ancient of all things that we consider "human". The emotional journey we embark on with every "once upon a time" takes us to another land where we forget ourselves and suspend rationality. Within the context of a story a seed is planted—we adopt the idea as our own and so the seeds of persuasion are planted.

The ancient Greek and Roman mythologies were stories of explanation. They were ways for people to understand the universe based on heroic stories and quests. The late author Joseph Campbell explains that myths help us to realize the wonder of the universe and our place in it; they also validate the customs and social rules of our culture. Myths are not just bedtime stories, they are more than that. They teach valuable lessons as well as entertain. The subjects discussed often entail the most human of all concerns: birth, life, death, and the battle of good and evil. Our modern lives are not far removed from this tradition of myth. Every movie, advertisement, book or popular piece of fiction tells a story. When we listen to these tales we suspend all belief and lose ourselves. This is why movies are so enjoyable— the loss of self -awareness while being fixated on something outside of you. These stories contain similar elements: characters, settings and plots. The stories usually involve a battle between characters representing opposing social values. The battle ensues and eventually a winner emerges, this winner is usually embodied by a product in advertising or an idea in rhetoric.

Through the medium of the story, values are transmitted that communicate what the story's creator wants to say. The message isn't obvious but rather quite subtle. The creator of the story taps into our conceptual inventory—our images, symbols, ideas, experiences and feelings. This creative world of ideas, values, images and emotions often escapes the rational analysis of our brains and thus a seed is planted—the seed of persuasion. Every story involves persuasion; persuading you to believe and hope that something is possible or to think in another way. Each commercial you watch is a little myth unfolding before you. It operates not on the realm of conscious attention but at a deeper level. Consumer psychology author Sal Randazzo explains it best:

"Each advertisement or commercial represents an individual mythology, which also contributes to the overall brand mythology. Megabrand advertising doesn't just sell a product; it creates an emotional bond between the brand and the consumer. Advertising creates this bond by mythologizing the product; by humanizing it; and by giving the product a distinct identity, personality, and sensibility. Advertising mythologizes brands by wrapping them in consumers' dreams and fantasies. "

The ancient Greeks used rhetoric to appeal to man's higher cognitive faculties. A superior argument would no doubt win the mental battle and demand submission from the less-skilled foe. Those who possessed the weapons of oration and superior linguistic ability could only administer this mental beat down. However, the weapons of persuasion aren't limited only to a rationally minded rhetoric approach. Myths serve to form the most powerful method of social compliance.

We tell stories about everything we do. We tell stories about who we are and what we want. Our stories are not static entities but instead flow like a child's imagination, bending and weaving with each moment. They are adaptable, unpredictable and emotional. We exist within a web of interconnected meaning, which we have placed on all things. We don't know why we do certain things, but, if asked, we can throw together an elaborate story, which, upon creation, strengthens a conviction in itself that cannot be readily shaken. Others also share this affinity. We are quick to judge but rarely do we afford ourselves the same critical eye. We think we know others but we only know them through the context of our own story. This story is the narrative and myth that we create for ourselves every second of every day. Within the contours of these myths and stories lie countless opportunities to be persuaded. Our stories don't exist alone but involve other actors; we cannot have a play without others. It is in this interaction with others that we are given opportunities to persuade. We may elect to use rhetoric or simply appeal to someone's emotions—the results are the same. This book is a story of persuasion. It is an introduction to the world of social compliance.

Persuasion and Your Brain

The methods that will be explained are used by all of us and many are used constantly against us. We may think we are immune to the effects of persuasion but, unfortunately, it just isn't true. However, there is hope, in the form of knowledge. Understanding how persuasion works will give you not only the ability to persuade others but also the ability to spot the techniques of persuasion a mile away. Whether you like it or not, we are all players in this game. Either we use these methods on others (which we already do) or have them used on us.

Our short journey into the world of persuasion will also provide some insight as to how our brains operate. The assumptions and processes we use to make decisions are standard across cultures and provide a glimpse into an evolutionarily adapted system of cognition. To simplify— persuasion works because our brains use automatic processes to categorize, catalog and judge the world, all for a very important reason. Simplicity. Our brains are pattern detection machines that work to simplify the world into cognitive rules of thumb called heuristics. These rules of thumb provide a framework for us to effectively navigate a world of endless stimuli and social complexities. We may look down on these processes that make us all susceptible to bias, stereotyping and judgments but they provide the foundation for us to operate smoothly. Without this streamlined process we would be forced to exhaust our limited cognitive faculties on every decision.

Like our myths and stories, the interplay between reality and our cognitive processes provides gaps that a cunning social compliance expert can use to insert an idea or opinion. The metaphorical wrench that gets thrown into the gears and wheels of our mental shortcuts can cause us to accept circumstances or conditions that an otherwise rational analysis would balk at. This sabotage of our mental processes is how we become victims of successful social compliance. By reading this book you will learn more about your brain and how easily you are fooled.

How to Use This Book

This book contains twenty-four of the most powerful methods of persuasion. Each explanation is a mixture of personal story, research, experimental results and psychology. Keep in mind that each persuasion technique is more than just a tactic; it represents the trap door to a larger, hidden way of how we process information and create value in our world. As you learn about each method, focus on the bigger picture. Ask yourself, *What does this persuasion technique teach me about how my brain evaluates information ?*

Each section contains a sample dialogue or situation that involves the bias. At the end there is an exercise that you must complete, identifying all the methods of persuasion in action. *Enjoy.*

Foot in the Door Technique: When You Just Ask For A Little

Son: Dad, can I borrow the car to go to John's house?

Father: Sure, but be careful.

Son: Thanks Dad. Do you think I could borrow it next weekend for a little road trip?

Want to get someone to do something for you? Start small. This is one of the classic compliance techniques; it involves a small request followed by a larger one. Asking someone for a larger request off the bat will most likely be met with rejection. The initial request may be a singular event or a series of escalating demands that slowly ramp up the commitment and allow the requester to eventually ask for a favor, which, relatively speaking, doesn't seem so large. The technique owes its success to what social scientists call "successive approximations". The basic premise is that the more a subject continues to oblige demands the resulting behavioral change will make him or her feel obligated to go along with larger requests.

The foot in the door technique is incredibly powerful for another, more devious, reason. Although the initial request may be granted simply due to the need to appear polite and respectful, subsequent requests can trigger a belief that you actually like the requester or want to help them. In an attempt to justify the decision to ourselves of why we helped them, it becomes easy to convince ourselves of a willingness that previously didn't exist. We can become committed to their cause.

Imagine allowing three random men into your home to

conduct a two-hour examination of household products for marketing research. Would you allow this? If you are like most of us, probably not. A study conducted in California[i] examined the effectiveness of the foot in the door technique. A team of researchers called housewives in California and asked them a few questions about household products; several days later they called again but with a different request. They asked if five or six men could conduct the two-hour examination. Results showed that women who agreed to answer a fifteen-minute survey were more than twice as likely to agree to the request than those who didn't.

I understand that a two-hour examination of all your personal grooming products along with whatever embarrassing ointments and gels you may have lying around seems excessive. How about a giant billboard on your lawn? Another study set out[ii] to determine if people would be willing to do this. The method was simple— initially contact homeowners and ask them if they wanted to install a smaller sign on their lawn. The researchers used a pro-social aspect and informed homeowners they would be promoting driver safety. The later request to have a giant sign put on their lawn was accepted by seventy-six percent of homeowners.

Even simply having people fill out a questionnaire about organ donation increased the willingness of participants to become organ donors. Research showed[iii] that increasing the length of the questionnaire wasn't followed by increased donation rates; just taking the survey was enough. Charities have caught on to this and apply it directly into door-to-door marketing campaigns. In one study participants were first asked to sign a petition before being prompted to make a donation to the organization. A second follow up group was not asked to sign the petition. Two weeks later canvassers asked homeowners to make a contribution to a local charity. Results were startling; simply signing a petition caused a dramatic increase in donations.

So why does the foot in the door technique work so marvelously? The answer lies in self-perception theory. The basic premise of the theory is that people want to exhibit behavior that aligns with their values. If they see themselves as generous, caring and helping people they will want to exhibit behavior that conforms to those standards. Compliance experts ask for a little request, which is followed by another one and eventually concluded with a larger demand. People end up complying with further requests once they have initially helped due to an internal created need to appear consistent.

So the next time someone tries to ask you for a little favor first, remember it might be the first step on a path that you would otherwise be unwilling to go down.

Bait and Switch: When What You See Isn't What You Get

Example 1: A car sales showroom displays a basic car outside with an extremely low price-tag. Potential customers see the low price and ask the salesman about the car. Once they have inquired and are seated in a sales office, a more expensive model is shown.

Just as the name implies, some form of enticing bait is used to drawn in consumers to a purchase. This could be the promise of a low price, a free product or an upgrade. Once customers have shown interest this is enough to start a high-pressure sales routine where customers are offered a more expensive version. Couple this with an aggressive sale style and someone who gives in easily and you have a wonderful recipe to dramatically increase sales.

This method is effective and some people are so susceptible to it that it's actually illegal. In the United States courts, purveyors of the bait and switch technique may be subject to lawsuit on the premise of false advertising. There is one loophole though; advertising a product while purposely limiting the supply, therefore causing it to sell out, isn't illegal. This is why you often see so many signs indicating "only for a limited time"; not only does it encourage people to buy via perceived scarcity but also gives salespeople an excellent method to bait and switch.

The psychology of the bait and switch is simple. When a person sees an initial item of high value priced low they cognitively "accept" the idea of acquiring it. This transition from a negative position to total commitment is not taken back easily. Once we have committed to ourselves that we actually want something we need to satisfy that feeling. Subsequent retraction of that initial offer will create an anxiety state, which people often feel they need to remedy by making concessions to purchase the more expensive item. If you're thinking this sounds suspiciously similar to a child, you're right! The little kid inside you is shouting, "I want it! I want it!" and can only be satisfied by getting something of equal interest.

In a 1989 study[iv], Joule and Weber used this method, which they referred to as the lure procedure. They invited a large group of students to watch interesting films and then tricked them into memorizing long lists of numbers. Unsurprisingly, when first asked to memorize numbers only 15 % agreed (who would agree to that?) but when prompted with a movie watching opportunity 47% agreed.

Have you ever been at a store simply browsing and felt the piercing gaze of the sales associate right behind you? You can feel they are watching you ready to pop up at any second with an overly friendly, "Can I help you?" The bait and switch is such a common practice, despite being illegal, that we have ALL at some point been victim to it. Let's examine some signs of a bait and switch in action.

1. . It's way too good to be true. I'm sure we have all heard of this term, if it's too good to be true it probably is. This well-meaning piece of pessimistic advice generally holds true for most situations. If you see a price that is so absolutely low, please listen to the rational side of your brain and realize that you can't finance a car for ninety-nine dollars a month. Unless a company is going out of business the next day, rock-bottom prices won't help them

generate revenue.

2. . Read the fine print or don't. I don't read the fine print. Ever. One, because it's *fine*, meaning that it's way too small. Two, because there is way too much *fine print* to be fine. The problem is unscrupulous merchants often use fine print to circumnavigate the legality involved in baiting and switching. It's their method of saying, "Hey, I'm not responsible for the misunderstanding! It's all there in the super small, barely legible, faded black ink!" A large amount of disclaimers are a good indication of this, legitimate businesses will also make such disclosures, however not to the extent of retailers using the bait and switch.

3. . Confusing price terms. Often we aren't shown the final price but rather an initial base price where taxes, add-ons and upgrades are added. The final price can be much different than we initially thought. One especially poignant example is car dealers who use this method to advertise monthly payments. Dealers attempt to distract buyers from learning the full details and length of the payment term. Once interest is shown a multitude of other features is added on.

4. . Deals are final. Unless you are buying ground beef, this is a telling sign of a disingenuous sales tactic. Sales are non-refundable and contact with the seller is often difficult. Stay away from these.

5. . Out of stock. Product A that you initially saw in the newspaper and wanted so badly you drove to the store to buy is out of stock. Luckily, you can buy

product B—a more expensive version of Product A also made in China.

6. . Financing. Be careful. If you are one of those, "I'm not so good with numbers," kinda people this is a serious trap. You might rope yourself into a terrible decision that haunts you for the next ten years. Although financing can be a convenient way for people to make larger purchases, such as homes and cars, it can be used by unsavory salespeople to rope in inexperienced customers. By offering a financing option at zero percent in the advertisement they often attract people with below average credit. They may inform you that the zero-credit option is only available for people with exceptionally good credit. Conceding to pay an increased financing rate for something you want is extremely dangerous.

So the next time you are offered an exceptionally good deal on something, be careful. Don't take the bait.

Door in the Face Technique: When You Go Big Than Go Small

Can you help me do this work?

Well, can you help me do some of it?

Mom, can I borrow 100?

Well, how about 20?

First you get a no then you get a yes. The request may involve the buyer slamming the door in his or her face, hence the name—door in the face technique. The first request made is so abrupt and over the top that it is immediately rejected. The following request is made immediately afterward while the taste of the first still lingers. The effect is that people often feel guilty about refusing another person and fear rejection as a result. The second request gives them an opportunity to make a small concession, which mitigates any threats of social rejection. However, in the end you might be doing something you otherwise wouldn't.

This also activates the contrast principle (when an event is judged in relation to a previous event). By making a larger request the smaller one pales in comparison and seems almost trivial. What is ten dollars when compared to a hundred?

The majority of us believe we are people who would help a person in need. For this reason the door in the face triggers an ingrained sense of social responsibility. An experiment[v] involving the effectiveness of the DITF technique demonstrated this. Researchers separated volunteers into three groups. In group 1, participants were first asked to volunteer to counsel juvenile delinquents for two hours a week for two years (yes, two years). This request was later followed up by a smaller request to accompany juvenile delinquents. The second and third groups were given equally small initial requests later followed by a slightly larger request to accompany minors. The results showed that the group first asked to take care of delinquents for two years was fifty percent MORE likely to help. This is a massive increase in compliance for a task that most people would steer away from entirely.

So the next time you want a raise you might want to ask your boss for an absurdly high amount first. If it doesn't work at least you know the principle of the DITF technique might ensure a better amount than just asking for it straight away. So, naturally, it works well for money but how about homework? Can assigning a huge initial load of homework force students to comply and do more homework than they would normally be comfortable with? An experiment looking at compliance techniques for children found that the DITF technique was extremely effective. The study[vi] involved three groups of 2nd grade students. The first group was asked by a teacher to do an easy fifteen-question worksheet and then asked fifteen minutes later to complete a twenty-minute worksheet. The second group was asked to first fill out a hundred-question worksheet. After refusal of the one hundred-page worksheet the group was asked to complete twenty questions. Results were measured by measuring quality of work, amount of help needed and overall mathematical ability. Results showed that the second group completed worksheets more effectively and needed less help.

Now, you may be thinking the door in the face sounds very similar to the foot in the door technique and you're right. Not only do they both involve doors and human body parts, they are both just as effective at increasing compliance in a variety of tasks. The next time you are trying to persuade someone remember that the key to success is to start making requests whether big or small. Either way you are embarking on the path of persuasion.

The Low Ball: When You Still Buy Even Through You Don't Want It

You are looking for a new vacation package. You choose a trip to Mexico and head into the sales office. During the inquiry you make a verbal commitment to purchase the trip to Mexico if the price is right. The salesman says, "OK," and goes to finalize the deal. He returns with a sad face, informing you that the Mexico trip is still available but because of the airline the price is now double. You still buy it.

The low-ball technique is the sleaziest of the sleaziest. It conjures an image of a jewelry clad, overweight used car salesman dressed in an oversized, half-open, Hawaiian T-shirt. The low ball is dirty but it's unfortunately effective. It works like this. The salesperson first gets closure and commitment to the idea or item that they want the other person to eventually purchase and then, using the fact that people will behave consistently with their personal beliefs, they will basically force the sale upon us. We want to sustain our commitment and dislike appearing indecisive. Whether we know it or not, there is also a powerful illusion of irrevocability where we believe that once a decision is made and verbally agreed upon it cannot be taken back. This is especially true if some finalizing act is committed— like a signature or even a handshake. As exciting as a handshake can be, the prospect of getting something new and shiny can create excitement, which, when followed by disappointment requires an immediate remedy—buying the next best thing. You might think to yourself, *I'm already here, I may as well.* No you shouldn't!

So the question is, if you are getting the ol' low ball, should you walk right out? Social obligation often prevents us from doing so and, God forbid, if the salesman gave us something like a coffee or a free soda we would feel obliged to stay. A 1978 study[vii] demonstrated a similar effect; two groups of students were asked to participate in an experiment. One group was told the experiment would start at 7am before they agreed, the second was asked to commit first then told the starting time. Despite being an exceptionally early time for most college students, fifty-six percent of the low-ball group agreed while only twenty-four percent of the other group agreed. Researchers found that when a person believes that they have made a free and non-coerced agreement they are even more willing to comply to an otherwise unacceptable condition.

So what is the difference between low ball and bait and switch? They are extremely similar but differ in their usage. Low ball is used for a single transaction depending on the individual. If the salesperson assesses the low-ball technique to be effective with that particular customer it may be employed. The bait and switch is embedded into advertisements and often used as a systematic method of selling different products.

The Closure Principle: How Insane Pressure Wins

So you don't want to buy this? Well, why did you come in and ask me the price? How about another product? Try this one. It's our bestseller. Don't you like it? How much are you willing to spend? Give me a number.

Insane pressure creates tension, we seek release from tension. This is the closure principle and it's simple—hound and annoy another person until they finally succumb and give in. One of the interesting facts about experiencing tension is that we seek resolution almost immediately; whether we run away or just coalesce, the result is the same—resolution. This is akin to the fight or flight reaction. There is a biological imperative to end the painful stimulus and doing so usually gives you a nice boost of brain opiates in the form of endorphins.

This is perhaps why mysteries or thrillers are so compelling. You just need to watch to the end, what will happen? Not only are you curious but also there is a need for closure, to see the thing through. Buying an item creates tension in the form of wanting. I want the object and the release of tension I seek comes in the form of the purchase.

That feeling of being pushed to the edge is exhilarating and a good salesperson can mimic that feeling. Think of going down a roller coaster, the adrenaline surging through your body as you slowly edge over the highest point. The excitement of a race or a sports game is another example. You may find yourself standing up shouting at the TV like it's a real person. Last minute tension can be intense and we want that point of finality.

It's important to note that, not only in this example but also in every compliance tactic, the emotional part of the brain takes over and when it does you can say goodbye to logic. The emotional brain's circuitry takes precedence and in a high stress environment we cannot think clearly. Closure fills in gaps using the primary tool of assumption. When faced with a situation we don't entirely understand, or when we don't have all the details, it's like connecting a terribly drawn dotted line. We seldom receive full information and in a situation where pressure is high we fill in those gaps by making assumptions. Let's say we want to buy a new appliance. It's a high-pressure situation. We neglect to ask important questions about some of its settings and warranty, assuming that the appliance will be OK.

I'm sure we can all think of a situation where we have agreed to something simply out of wanting to escape pressure. We may not realize it but this is the closure principle in action. We may justify our reaction as just being nervous or—even more likely and sinister yet—convince ourselves that we actually wanted the forced decision. The next time you are put into a situation of high pressure, stop and think. Is the decision you are about to make truly your own or is it a product of the need for resolution, an escape from perceived danger? If you build tension in another person, they will seek closure or just hate you for it.

Authority Principle: When You Do What the Guy with the Uniform Says

If a security guard came up to you on the street and told you to do something, would you? What if the security guard's uniform looked like he bought it for five dollars at a local second hand thrift shop?

I would bet that you'd listen to him. Not only would you listen to him but most of us would obey unquestionably. We see the uniform and our instant response is to comply. This is the authority principle. Symbols of authority activate an instant need to obey. The uniform of a policeman, the coat of a doctor or someone's title are all powerful vehicles for authority. The principle works in two ways. First, we will obey without thinking and, second, we don't permit ourselves to challenge it.

Who was the first authority figure in your life? Probably not a policeman, unless for some odd reason you live in a house of policemen. Our first authority figures are usually our parents, normally our mothers. We are trained from a young age to obey authority; first our parents then our teachers then policemen and, finally, our employers. This is the authority evolution scale and it works in all countries regardless of cultural upbringing. It becomes an easy way to understand the world. We divide people into two categories, those who are superior to us (have authority over us) and those who aren't (we have authority over them). This is an effective way for a child to understand the world and serves the need to simplify everything. Only during adolescence do we become aware of the idea of rebellion and seek to purposely disobey authority figures.

Authority is really about trust. We want to trust another person to guide us in what to do. The sad truth is that most of us don't want to think for ourselves all the time. We want that figure in our lives to guide us and provide the message that implies, "Don't worry, everything is under control. Just listen to me." When we aren't willing to take control of everything in our own lives we look to others to provide that control and direct us.

One of the most famous experiments displays this. The infamous Milgram[viii] experiment involved a large group of students who were told they were participating in an experiment to test pain. Subjects were put into an isolated room where they would control electric shocks given to an actor in an adjacent room. The electric apparatus had a setting marked in red with "XXXX" for a final, potentially deadly dose of electricity. The researchers, wearing white lab coats and carrying clipboards, instructed students to continually give shocks despite the actor crying out in pain. This continued until the actor was screaming for the electric shocks to stop, in one case even mentioning a pre-existing heart condition. The majority of students carried on with the electric shocks well into the XXX zone. Milgram concluded from this experiment that humans possess an "extreme willingness … to go to almost any lengths on the command of an authority." Now let me ask you what would you do? Remember logical and emotional processes don't work together.

Before the experiment, researchers did a survey[ix] amongst a range of psychology and sociology professors asking what the predicted compliance rate would be. The majority predicted an extremely low rate of about five percent. The actual result of an over ninety percent compliance rate was shocking. This is also based on the fact that the researcher identified himself as a researcher and wore the appropriate symbol of authority—a uniform.

Another example of this authority is perhaps even more frightening. In this experiment a man called on duty nurses at a local hospital, identifying himself as a doctor in another department. This doctor gave instructions for medication administration—a medication that was still being tested, was dangerous and could only be used in small quantities. Despite knowing the instructions were clearly wrong, the nurses didn't use their own clinical judgment. The alleged doctor's orders were followed ninety-five percent of the time. Luckily for the patient's sake, a confederate was hiding in the room ready to stop the injection from actually happening. There have also been examples of this on airlines where crew or copilots have withheld objection about a potentially dangerous decision by the captain, sometimes leading to disaster.

Obeying authority is, in most cases, a good idea. You should probably listen to the doctor. You should probably listen to the lawyer. You should probably listen to your teacher. In most situations it serves us well to listen to authority figures and we learn this fact early. However, when the symbols of authority are adopted for more nefarious or commercial purposes people can become influenced without even being aware of it.

The symbols of authority are many and we will examine them in the next few paths to persuasion. This isn't a call to reject all forms of authority but rather to understand how susceptible we are to the symbols of it. It also represents a very primal need in humans to be governed and controlled. We want someone to provide the control and security that is otherwise absent in an unpredictable life.

Clothing: We Are All Superficial

You get into the elevator. On the next floor a sharply dressed business man enters the elevator. He has a pressed shirt and designer watch. You don't know what he does but his clothing implies a sense of professionalism and wealth.

If you are what you eat then, to the world, you are how you dress. The passerby who only has one to two seconds must use the most powerful evidence to assess you —your clothing. I know it's quite superficial but, unfortunately, appearances provide a quick decision making tool when time is limited. In the realm of authority, clothing is a powerful symbol.

In complex societies, there are a wide variety of positions and social interactions we must successfully navigate through. Each person's respectable position in society requires a different level of communication. One may reserve formal communication for strangers and work associates but use a casual style of communication for closer relationships. Each social position has an expected set of behavior. Part of this expected behavior is how we dress. Clothing is directly linked to social positions and authority. It also acts as a powerful communicator and often forms the basis for interaction. This is demonstrated by the reception a man in a well-dressed suit will receive over another wearing only shorts. Therefore clothing often sets the stage for successful social interaction and acknowledgment of authority.

A 1990 experiment[x] conducted by Mary Lynn Damhorst tested this hypothesis. She conducted an analysis of 190 impression formation studies (basically showing people pictures) to determine what kind of information was communicated by clothing. She found that in the majority of her studies (81%) the meaning and information most frequently communicated was competence, power and intelligence. These social markers of authority were the first to be picked up on; a powerful example of our hyper-sensitivity to authority conveying messages.

The kind of car you drive has always been a popular indicator of wealth and status. Like clothing, driving an expensive luxury vehicle displays a powerful example of power and wealth. If asked, would you treat a man in an expensive car differently from another man in a cheaper car? Most of us would say we wouldn't. Despite wanting to be fair, studies have shown that most of us hold an unconscious deference for such vehicles. A study conducted[xi] in San Francisco found that "owners of luxury auto cars received a special kind of deference from others." This research was based on the observation that motorists at stoplights would honk more readily for owners of normal economy vehicles versus owners of expensive luxury vehicles.

We would like to think that we aren't superficial and don't use clothing as criterion for decision making but, unfortunately, when time is limited we often resort to our biased mental shortcuts—in this case, deference to symbols of authority.

Reactance: Don't Tell Me How to Live My Life

Billy's parents told him he can't go out this weekend. Billy wasn't even planning on doing anything this weekend and had no particular plans. However, the action of his parents forbidding him to go out has unleashed an inner need to fight his parents' attack on his freedoms. Billy sees himself as an independent person and doesn't want to be restrained by others.

When others tell you what to do or not to do, we make a concerted effort to act in opposition. If our freedom to choose an action is threatened, we get a powerful feeling called "reactance". Think of when you were a rebellious teenager fighting all your parents' wishes, proclaiming, "They just don't understand me." Rewind to a time earlier, the notorious "terrible twos" is characterized by a period where infants are learning the power of autonomy and the need to react to gain control over that autonomy. As we get older reactance takes a backseat in our decision-making but it can still be an extremely powerful persuader. As we study the effects and use of reactance, keep in mind that its power lies in the ability to convince yourself that the desire to commit to a certain action is perceived to be internally generated. Good persuasion always starts with convincing yourself that it's your own idea, not someone else's.

So if I told you to do something, would you comply? Or would you feel an increased need to tell me to go away and mind my own business? We don't like things limiting our freedoms, especially if we are American. We react against anything that threatens it, real or imaginary. Have you ever met someone who could be described as hypersensitive—a person who reacts to every perceived threat with hostility, even though the actions or words directed at them are not meant to undermine their freedoms? This is reactance. There is almost a sense of naughty enjoyment in breaking the rules and flaunting imposed power and doing what we want. Think about being in love; the classic story of *Romeo and Juliet* is a great example of reactance. How much more likely are people to fall in love and develop a stronger bond when encountering parental interference? The more parents resist the stronger the bond grows. This works for teenagers who are told not to take drugs or smoke. The label of disapproval and taboo create an even stronger desire to engage in the prohibited action.

When we make things illegal they somehow become more enticing. Whenever someone is heavily pressured into accepting a certain view or attitude, reactance can cause the subject to adopt or strengthen a view or attitude that is contrary to what was intended. It also increases resistance to persuasion. Now, you may be wondering how this is a form of persuasion if it involves moving away from conformity, but the answer is simple—it works in reverse. It's called reverse psychology and it's when we attempt to influence someone to choose the opposite of what they request. Put more concisely, when I offer a freedom-limiting option the natural reaction will be resistance to conformity and an eventual decision to do the opposite of my request; which is exactly what I want. If reactance can be accurately predicted, a compliance expert can convince you to move in opposition of your request but, unbeknownst to you—straight to their real goal. *Tricky. Tricky.*

Reactance is so stubborn and powerful because there is a

powerful, emotionally driven motive not to be controlled by others. Even when subject to a tactic of reverse psychology, the resistance to a particular idea can be almost fanatical. We become even more entrenched in our opinion and perspective. The level of reactance is also flexible. The more important the free behavior being threatened the greater the magnitude of the reactance. Therefore reactance varies in relation to what is perceived to be under attack.

In one of the most illuminating studies of reactance, a 1977 study[xii] by Brehm and Weintraub exposed twenty four-month-old children to equally attractive toys. A large Plexiglas barrier separated all the toys. The first group had a barrier that was short enough to be reached over to grab whatever toy they wanted. The second group wasn't as lucky; their barrier was too high to reach over. To get the toys they would have to walk around the barrier. Results showed that when presented with an obstacle children were more than three times as likely to want to walk around the barrier and get the toy.

How about adults? A 1975 study[xiii] by the same researchers conducted an experiment on the campus of the University of North Carolina. Students were given a speech favoring coed dorms being banned. Worchel, Arnold, and Baker (1975)[xiv] examined the attitudes of University of North Carolina students before and after the speech favoring the banning of coed dorms. Students' opinions before the speech were pretty passive; no one really agreed or disagreed. However, a surprising change occurred after the speech; support for coed dorms increased by a massive amount in the otherwise passive population.

One sure fire method of getting a lot of attention is telling people they shouldn't do something or need to be careful. Another experiment by Zellinger, Fromkin, Speller and Kohn [xv] tested this by showing undergraduates advertisements for a novel. For half the students the advertisement contained a disclaimer indicating,"A book for adults only, restricted to those 21 and over." The other half was not subject to this disclaimer. The results showed the efficiency of reactance; students who read the restriction wanted to read the book more and believed that they would like the book more than those who had not read the disclaimer. Simply put, when stuff is censored it just makes us want to see it even more. I'm sure you can think of a few situations of this in your own life.

It is such a funny quirk of the human psyche that we are perennially drawn to the things that cause us harm. We are unconsciously drawn to the things that complicate our lives and make decisions that aren't in our best interests. Perhaps it's symptomatic of a deeper search for meaning masked by an outward need for drama. Either way that drama makes life both memorable and meaningful. Even in love the reactance effect comes into play. A 1972 study [xvi] interviewed 140 Colorado couples. Results showed that those experiencing a high degree of parental interference expressed a greater love for one another and were more seriously considering marriage. As you can clearly understand, this flavor of reactance has been dubbed the "Romeo and Juliet" effect.

Can you think of examples in your own life where "forbidden fruit" tempted you into an action or series of decisions that you wouldn't otherwise commit to? The best way to avoid this pervasive, powerful method of persuasion is simply to be mindful of our innate need to resist limitations on our freedoms. This is especially true for North Americans who have been raised on their inalienable right for this. We are hypersensitive to any perceived threat and quick to tell others, "Don't tell me how to live my life."

Another funny example comes to us from Dade County, Florida. A local ordinance decided to ban the use and possession of laundry detergents containing phosphates (basically most cleaning products). What do you think everyone did? Well, naturally they went out and bought all the possible phosphate detergent available, even raiding nearby counties for their supplies as well. Like teenagers resisting their parents' attempts at control, local residents went out of their way to acquire a ridiculous amount of detergent. Follow up surveys showed that residents held even more positive attitudes about the effectiveness of the detergent.

How about guns? Ironically, the recent media call to limit gun laws and impose harder restrictions on getting a gun has triggered a powerful reactance. Yes, unfortunately the demand for guns has increased. When local authorities attempt to limit our freedoms we get angry, but how does reactance affect us on a larger scale?

You might think wars are started by lack of resources. When times are tough the true cruel true human nature shows its ugly face and spurs us to kill our neighbors over their coveted resources. Actually this is not true. Researcher James Davis has found[xvii], "we are most likely to find revolutions where a period of improving economic and social conditions is followed by a short, sharp reversal in those conditions. Thus it is not the traditionally most downtrodden people--who have come to see their deprivation as part of the natural order of things--who are especially liable to revolt. Instead, revolutionaries are more likely to be those who have been given at least some taste of a better life." When what we have is taken away we react even harsher than when conditions are already depressed. This flies in the face of what most of us think is the common sense reason for conflict and strife.

Public debate and auctions are a great place to see reactance in action. The elements of competition, scarcity and reactance all blend together to make a wonderful recipe to make you do things you would otherwise never think of committing to. Barry Diller of ABC television found this out the hard way in an epic open-bid pricing war that led him to purchase a onetime showing of The Poseidon Adventure for 3.3 million. In case this doesn't seem extreme—it happened in 1973. One can only imagine the "What the hell have I done?" feeling that must have hit Mr. Diller after agreeing to the massive sum.

The next time someone tries to tell you what you can or can't do, remember that there is a hidden teenager waiting inside ready to shout, "Don't tell me what to do!" Reactance rears its ugly head whenever our freedoms are being restricted and encourages us to commit to courses of action that we wouldn't otherwise consider.

Altruism: When You Are Better Than That

I didn't know who to ask about this problem. I thought about it all day and then I remembered how kind you were to me last time. You are such a good person. Could you do this for me? I can't do it by myself.

Feeling like a good person is great, right? We get that surge of feel good serotonin that makes us feel proud of what we just did. Appealing to people's better nature is a powerful way to persuade others. Asking them to agree just because what you are asking is the "kind" thing to do works in two ways. First, you are setting an expectation of them and people naturally want to conform to this. Second, if they were not to do the "kind" action then that would imply they are somehow unkind. Altruism works by appealing to our good nature.

When we think of methods of persuasion we generally think of the more disingenuous methods like the low ball or the door in the face technique, but this assumptive approach is one of the most classic forms of persuasion. People enjoy being asked to help. Many people are unsure of when to start helping or if they should. There is a general distaste for people who infringe on our sense of autonomy. Another reason why the method of altruism works so well is that obliging to your request makes people more likely to help us in the future as well.

Although there is much debate as to the true essence of altruism (is it truly selfless or entirely selfish?) the point remains that it's a powerful ingrained trait of both biological and cultural evolution. Either way there is one simple fact—helping others feels great. A recent study showed that helping others can also increase one's sense of self-worth. The research foundxviii that giving emotional support to a partner increased the giver's positive mood. In general, research finds that social approval motivates helping. Another important aspect of this approach is to consider the desire to avoid punishments or distress for a lack of helping. Research has found that those who experience the most arousal in response to the distress of people are more likely to help those people.

I must mention one last important element of the appeal of altruism—the feeling of pride. Feeling good about one's achievements or just being a good, helpful person is an enticing reason to help others. When we succeed and feel good the natural reaction is to feel prouder and have a greater sense of self-worth. This is the opposite of feeling guilty or regretful for inaction. So let's look at this in action. Asking someone to help you do something that they might otherwise not do can create powerful feelings of pride and happiness that make them more than likely to help you again. Future action carries risk, which for some may paralyze them into inaction. By asking someone for help, the promise of future self-worth and pride contained within your appeal of "you are so kind I know you will help me" can conquer their paralyzing fear and make them do something they would otherwise not do.

So the next time you are struggling for some help, remember that you can always ask and the majority of people will help.

Negative Self Feeling: When You Don't Help You Feel Bad

I'm not sure that is a great idea, Steve. If you did that wouldn't you feel bad for not helping your friend? I think we should all be here for each other. It might make you feel good today but what about tomorrow?

The appeal to altruism hopes to spur people into action through the promise of feelings of self-worth and pride. Negative self-feelings work conversely; making people feel bad. Asking others to comply with your request and mentioning potential negative social impressions appeals to our inner need to be seen as "good". From childhood we are raised to mimic the virtues of the good boy or girl. These ideals carry on into adulthood where we strive to provide strong role models for our children. Implying that a certain action will be negative appeals to our inner need to be seen as good. This can be achieved by indicating that disagreeing with you could be wrong or bad or that others may suffer as a result of your actions.

For people lacking in self-confidence and self-worth this can be a powerful method of compliance. Imagine if you were already feeling bad about yourself and someone started to mention the idea of "this isn't you" or that's not the "real you". These statements can hit home in a hard way. Appealing to one's deepest sense of personal worth through the use of fear mongering tactics of shame, regret or alienation are shameful tactics.

We discussed the theory of self-perception earlier—the idea that actions that don't conform to our values create a sense of cognitive dissonance (feeling bad). This is a prime example. Implying that another person is acting against his or her values will create an inner battle of cognitive dissonance. A slightly altered version of what we have done creates a gap between our actions and beliefs. This is especially powerful if used by a persuasive personality or orator. Someone who can eloquently sweep us off our feet with his or her words or power of speech can start to make us question ourselves. If this seems too abstract, let's examine a sample dialogue.

Bob: I saw that you didn't finish the project the other day. Don't you think that the boss will be disappointed or even a little angry that you didn't complete it? I think you don't care about your job here.

Susan: Of course I care. I just couldn't finish it.

Bob: You know if you cared enough you would do it. You said you would work harder. This isn't a good example.

I hope this conversation doesn't sound familiar but we can see two powerful examples here. The first is the mention that not completing the project will lead to disappointment or even anger. The second is when Bob points out that Susan's actions were in contradiction to her values. She has no choice but to feel guilty and think less of herself as her self-worth declines.

Negative self-feelings remind me of a nagging mother, one who is constantly unsatisfied with your performance and if you drop your guard for a second her passive aggressive comments can actually hit their target. When people mention our mistakes and inconsistencies it can make us feel compelled to equivocate and defend our position or, worse yet, feel guilty about our actions. There are times when this is appropriate but when used as a form of social compliance these references to character flaws and inconsistencies are malicious and are intended for one purpose—the purpose of making you feel bad enough to change your own behavior.

Pleading Principle: When You Beg

Please John. Help me. You are so much more experienced and better at this than I am. If you don't help me I simply can't do it. I don't have the background that you have.

This isn't asking, this is begging. Most people avoid begging and some would rather face extreme consequences than lower themselves to begging. Lowering yourself is exactly the point of this persuasion method.

Have you ever walked by a person begging on the road? You choose to ignore them, help them out or think why don't get a job. Begging is a direct plea to our sense of social status. When you beg you put yourself into an inferior social position, showing that you are not a threat and you require someone else's help. Our culture demands that people who are in inferior positions must be helped. Those who help are given status and power; in exchange they must concede to the request. Simply put, vulnerable people should be protected.

In a sense praying is a form of pleading. Any appeal to a higher authority to help us is an example of pleading. It is often believed that the greater the display of sincerity the more likely that the deity will answer his or her prayers. The same often goes for relationships; women may use a childlike voice and even produce fake tears all in an attempt to invoke a sense of parental duty. The man will often react accordingly, feeling obliged to help the "child".

Ingratiation: When You Get Others to Like You

Judy has just transferred departments. She has befriended several staff members; however, her favorite person is Monica. Monica is a sales manager and holds a position slightly higher than Judy's. Judy is new to the office but almost everyone already likes her. She is quick to compliment others on their appearance or skill level, often asking for their advice on matters. She listens intently and agrees with all the advice she receives. Every Friday she also brings in an exceptionally large batch of cookies for everyone in the office.

Who doesn't like nice things being said about them, especially when it's in front of others? Ingratiation can be described in three different methods: flattery, agreement, and self-presentation. Each method attempts to stroke the person's ego or sense of identity and eventually they want to repay you for your kindness. People who have a weaker self-image are often more apt to succumb to the effects of this persuasion method.

Flattery is the act of commending someone for his or her achievements, abilities or outward appearance. It is particularly effective if used in a social situation where it provides a sense of social proof to someone's worth. Agreement is demonstrated in a concerted effort to show others that you agree with them. People like others who agree with them. Aligning with their opinions and ideas serves as a powerful way to build a lasting bond with another person. Even physically matching their body posture and stance can create this bond. Notice the next time you are talking how naturally we adopt the pose of a more prominent person or how they adopt ours. We may be standing with our arms crossed and before long they are also mimicking the same position. This is not coincidental but rather an example of our innate need to create social bonds through "agreement". Excellent socializers are like social chameleons—they are quick to adapt and align themselves, if only temporarily, with those around them.

Self-presentation is the last element of ingratiation. Simply put, we like people who look like us. Presenting yourself in a similar way to the person you are with is a great way to accomplish this. Presenting yourself as a person willing to listen and show genuine effort in trying to get to know them will create a similarly powerful bond.

The entire point of all three methods is similarity. Appearing as someone similar to the person we are trying to know creates social bonds. Similarity breeds familiarity. This is why we often mention a fact related to a person's interest. Oh you like badminton? My cousin is a professional badminton player. As inconsequential as this may seem, it still serves to build a bond.

When we discuss these methods outright there can be a somewhat sleazy or disingenuous feeling. Flattery and methods of ingratiation seem fake and superficial when they are used too obviously. When we know another person's motives it can be viewed with distaste. However, ingratiation truly works when we aren't aware of the motive. The key to successful ingratiation is when the person doesn't realize what you're doing. This implies a sense of subtleness over exaggeration. Even though you may deny it, flattery works on all manner of people. Those with high self-esteem and opinion of themselves enjoy flattery because it aligns with their self-view. Ironically, those with the lowest self-esteem also enjoy flattery because it acts as a boost even though they may not agree.

If someone is an extremely experienced flatterer they will often employ a criticism first-compliment after method. The contrast between the criticism and the compliment make it all the more powerful. Now let's look at some examples of flattery in action.

The world's greatest salesman is a man named Joe Girardxix who sold 13,001 cars at a Chevrolet dealership between 1963 and 1978. His method was simple; he would send out cards to each of his former 13,000 customers that said, "I like you." That was it, the simplest form of a compliment possible. The power of flattery was also revealed in a North Carolina study that tested the effects of positive, mixed and negative comments made to male subjects. The results showed that, despite knowing the person giving the compliment stood to gain from their liking him and that the comments of pure praise were entirely fictitious, they were just as effective. In other words, positive comments produced just as much liking for the flatterer when they were untrue as when they were true.

So, in the end, remember that ingratiation is all about getting another person to form a bond with you. We feel loyalty and responsibility to those we have formed social bonds with. Flattery, agreement and self-appearance are all effective paths of persuasion to form that bond.

Reciprocity: When You Give Gifts

Just take it as a little gift of my appreciation. It didn't cost much, it's ok.

Want to get more from others? The answer is simple, give them gifts first. People feel obliged to repay your kindness even when it isn't asked for. You may be thinking of bribery but bribery involves an excessive gift for agreement to partake in an action that is ethically or professionally reprehensible. The rule of reciprocity works so effectively because it triggers ingrained social codes of conduct that are essential to existing within a community. The idea of the Golden Rule, to treat others as you would want to be treated, is a powerful modifier of human behavior. There is a societal disgust reserved for people who take without returning. These ungrateful people are disliked cross culturally and for good reason. The rule of reciprocity makes sharing possible. If there weren't a powerful social motivation to return favors you have received people would be less willing to share in the first place.

Reciprocity is about producing a sense of obligation to return a larger favor. The feeling of obligation allows an action to be reciprocated with another action, often of greater magnitude. Interestingly, this dynamic can serve to develop and continue relationships with people. Now, before you begin thinking that reciprocation is all about physical presents you should know that emotional gifts of invested time and energy work equally well. Reciprocation is about trust. The easiest definition of trust is a delayed exchange. If I do something for you today without asking for a return then I trust that you will one day repay the favor sometime in the future. Society without this element of trust must rely on a third party to ensure fair trade; this is what banks and lawyers are for.

So how can you apply this within your own life? Let's look at some real life examples of the reciprocity rule in action. In a 1971 experimentxx by Dennis Degan, subjects were asked to take part in an "art appreciation" experiment. During the experiment the researchers would leave the room for a two-minute break and bring back a soft drink for the students in the first group. After the art experiment was completed, the researchers asked subjects if they wanted to buy raffle tickets from him. In the second group the researcher behaved exactly the same but didn't bring subjects a soft drink. Results showed that subjects who had received the favor, a soft drink, bought more raffle tickets than those in the second group despite the fact that they didn't even ask for a drink. Regan also asked subjects to fill out a survey after they finished the experiment to find if they personally liked the researcher and if that had influenced their decision to buy more raffle tickets. The majority of students reported that the free coke hadn't affected their judgment in purchasing the raffle tickets; however, comparison of the two groups showed dramatically different results.

There are two interesting takeaways from this experiment. The first is that, despite being clearly influenced by receiving an unsolicited act of generosity, subjects were still not ready to believe the act had modified their behavior. They resisted the idea that they could be influenced by a simple gift, but they were. The second is even more salient, the emotional burden to repay bothers people so much that they overcompensate with more than was initially given.

This is not an isolated case; further experiments reveal the same idea. People given gifts will often respond with returns that are disproportionately large. Perhaps it's simply because we don't want to appear cheap, giving a gift of greater worth ensures we are seen as even more generous.

Another example of this involves the Hare Krishnas, a religious group who became very popular in the 1980s. Currently they are a very well funded and wealthy group with a well-diversified portfolio of investments and property, but this wasn't always the case. In the early 1980s the Krishnas were struggling for donations; as a charity they relied on disciples asking members of the public for donations. The problem was they weren't getting any donations; the solution came in the form of a simple flower. Devotees began giving a simple daisy to potential donators informing them, "This is our gift for you." Donations sky-rocketed. Not only did people give money but they gave more than previously experienced. We can see the same principle as the soft drink experiment repeated—giving more than you get.

Now let's not forget Amway, the network marketing system that swept through America in the 1990s. Amway sales were stagnating and, whether by genius or luck, they came upon a brilliant idea: giving prospects a package of sample products—cleaners, deodorizers, and insect killers. They called it the BUG. It worked like this. The distributor leaves a BUG within a prospect client's home for three days. No required cost or obligation, if they don't like it they can return it anytime. The only request made is that the homeowners try out the products. After this time period the representative returns to acquire the BUG and ask for a purchase. The sense of obligation for many homeowners is too great and the majority order on the spot. Having been given products to sample in such a generous way makes them feel obliged to return the favor. Amway representatives later reported sales were, "Unbelievable. We have never seen such excitement. Our products are moving at an unbelievable rate."

One of the most poignant examples of this in my own life occurred in Morocco. During a two-week vacation there with my mother we were shopping in a local bazaar. My mother was lured into one of the shops for some soap and fragrance products and began talking with the store clerk who soon offered her a cup of fresh mint tea. She looked at me and I quickly shook my head in disapproval. I knew what would happen if she accepted his "generous act" and, before long, when she wanted to go she couldn't. She felt obliged and, by way of compensation, bought way too much of the overpriced product. Being aware of the reciprocity rule allows us to see it everywhere. This fundamental rule of human evolution is one of the defining factors of being human. As noted anthropologist Richard Leakey once said, "We are human because our ancestors learned to share their food and their skills in an honored network of obligation."

Framing: When How You Say It Is All That Matters

May I please use the photocopier?

Hey, Rob. Do you think I could use the photocopier? I need to present something to the boss and I don't have much time.

Clearly, the second situation will result in a much higher compliance rate than the first. It's all about how you say it, or, in this case, frame it. Meaning depends on context. One thing can mean something radically different in another context, so control the context. Context is definitely king. We create meaning not just through our words but rather the interplay between our setting, mood and the other elements that surround us. Words are not isolated entities. When we change our surroundings the meaning of the main topic is also changed. Through effectively framing a request or question we can change its tone, validity and success rate.

The meaning of reality—the experiences, events, objects, processes and facts we encounter daily—is not set but dynamic. Tomorrow you might interpret an event entirely differently than you would right now. Our experiences are not absolute but rather contextual. The active construction of our realities leaves a lot of room for persuasion. We must decide: which parts are important? Which are relevant? How you position yourself gives you all the power in the world to persuade.

We do this naturally. If we want to convince someone to do something we first start with a detailed explanation of all the merits involved in doing so. We might want to convince our friend to try a new restaurant by informing him of the delicious food, beautiful women and affordable prices. Once the restaurant has been framed within this context convincing him will be much easier. This is just one small example of the way framing is used in a bigger context.

In 1981, famous researchers Amos Tversky and Daniel Kahnemanxxi explored how different phrasing could affect participants' responses about hypothetical life or death situations. Participants were asked to choose between two treatment options for six hundred people affected by a deadly disease. Treatment A involved 400 deaths, whereas treatment B had a 33 % chance that no one would die but a 66% chance that everyone would die. This choice was then presented to participants either with positive framing, i.e. how many people could potentially live, or negative framing, i.e. how many would perish. Which would you choose?

Treatment A was chosen by 72 % of participants when it was presented with positive framing (saving 200 lives) and dropped only to 22% when framed in a negative context (400 people will die). This framing effect has been replicated many times in multiple studies.

One area where the effects of framing are particularly rampant is the political arena. Politics requires a high level of persuasive ability and swaying public opinion is no easy feat, or is it? Politicians are masters at compliance and framing is one of their most cherished weapons. If a particular political agenda wants to be carried out then the simple precursor to this is emphasizing a related problem. Want people to support a new economic policy? Simply mention the employment rate and constantly mention unemployment rates. This also works in court cases too. Pretrial detention has actually been shown to increase the defendant's willingness to accept a plea bargain, since imprisonment, rather than freedom, is his baseline. Pleading guilty will be viewed as an event that will cause his earlier release rather than as an event that will put him in prison.

You don't become immune to framing as you get older. Just in case you were thinking, No one could fool me with this stuff, you are probably wrong. Studies show xxii that framing actually increases with age. "Another cause is that older adults have fewer cognitive resources available to them and are more likely to default to less cognitively demanding strategies when faced with a decision. They tend to rely on easily accessible information, or frames, regardless of whether that information is relevant to making the decision in question." Even learning a new language can make you susceptible to framing—lacking the fluency and ability to parse slight grammatical and contextual nuances creates a powerful opportunity for framing.

Framing is the mind's way of finding chaos in a sea of meaningless. By assigning meaning to events and context we create a roadmap to navigate the world—fulfilling a primary survival function. Simple statistics are perhaps the best at illustrating this. Consider these examples:

A 95 % effective condom appears more effective than one with a 5% failure rate.

People prefer to take a 5% raise when inflation is at 12% than take a 7% cut when inflation is zero.

Buying beef? People prefer a label indicating 80% lean over 20 % fat.

Since framing is such an active process of meaning creation, we can use this same method to powerful effect to re-frame our own problems. How about seeing your problems and fears as opportunities instead of actual problems? Not only can we use this method of compliance to persuade others but also ourselves.

Inference: When You Don't Say What You Want Them to Think

Person A: So I was looking at the project and realized that you were wrong.

Person B: So that means you were right?

We all know what inference is—a common literary device used in literature and daily life where logical conclusions are made based on previous premises that are assumed to be true. Another way to look at inference is as a logical observation of what facts are presented in a particular pattern. Our minds must make sense of what we experience; we rely on previous experience, values, mood, needs and goals to do this. We assign casual factors based on this wealth of internal data as we transition from an isolated rule to a more generalized one. This is why being late a few times can get you labeled as a perpetually "late" person. Our brains are excellent pattern detectors. We can take partial information and make a complete picture, a picture that is sometimes slightly skewed or entirely fictitious. Within this wiggle room of what is actually happening and what we perceive to be happening opens a large opportunity for persuasion.

The output of inference is meaning. In most cases this meaning is valid and we continue to make further use of it, but sometimes our assumptions are skewed towards some invalid meaning. If you are required to make an important decision but the party in charge of providing information only presents a biased perspective, you will make a natural inference that is invalid.

In the previous section I talked about someone trying to convince a man to go to a restaurant. He made mention of the good food, beautiful women and enjoyable environment. This is framing at its finest. Now, if the same person were to use inference it would go something like this:

Person A: I want to eat with you but I don't have much money and also can't go too far. (Both people know there is great Korean restaurant nearby)

Person B: Hmm. We could always go to that Korean restaurant nearby. It's cheap and not too far away.

Person A: Sure. I can do that.

Inference works and the trickiest part about it is that the victim has convinced himself or herself. The idea is internalized as their own not a third party's. This method of persuasion is so abstract and so subtle that it's even difficult to find research explaining it. Using skewed pre-planned circumstances or words to influence another person to infer a decision that is in your favor is the most powerful form of compliance in this book. When you come to your own conclusion you will defend that stance and idea vigorously.

An external idea that is internalized is like a parasite, a parasite you don't even know you have.

Scarcity: When You Want One Because There Might Only Be One

Person A: We should just buy the car now.

Person B: Don't rush. We just got here and we haven't had time to really think about it.

Person A: It's a great car. It's the only one here too. I want to get it before it's gone.

The principle of scarcity invokes that little kid inside you who just wants it because he wants it. In this case it's because you are thinking, I want it now because I might not be able to in the future. Suddenly something that was uninteresting becomes a must-have item. It's simple human psychology and exemplifies our prehistoric past where instant gratification ruled over delayed rewards. What is less available becomes more desirable. The utility of the item is not as important as the fact that it may soon not be within our possession.

Scarcity works not only on an evolutionary level but also an emotional level. It works through the anticipated regret, the regret we will experience when we think about the future and see ourselves regretting not having taken action. It's a current anxiety about an unpleasant future state. When we forecast the future we also experience expected emotional states.

Scarcity also falls within the realm of "prospect theory", which is our tendency to value a gain that is certain more than a gain that is less certain. We focus more on loss than gain. Warning people of what they will lose is often more effective than telling them about potential gains. An excellent example is weight loss—people generally only start trying to lose weight when they are told what they may lose (life/mobility).

If an object is seen as rare it must mean that it's inherently more valuable. This is most readily seen in the consumer realm, slapping a quick "limited number" tag on something is sure to make it sell out. This also works when implementing the deadline tactic—making time scarce. The scarcity principle also works well at making a person seem more attractive than usual; being in demand or unavailable can be enticing for some.

There is also an anticipation of social effects, especially the feeling of other people getting something when you can't. This competitive element makes us begin to imagine others getting an item while we are left on the sidelines. This feeling extends itself to a consideration of status—if another has an item and we don't, perhaps they will appear superior. This perceived inflation of value works especially well with information. Info that is harder to access and labeled "Secret" is more desirable and also perceived to be more correct. If we put ourselves through the hardship of acquiring a scarce item or piece of knowledge an interesting thing happens. Since we have gone through all the associated troubles of actually getting the item we become thoroughly convinced of its validity and utility.We discussed this earlier in the section about inference—the need to vehemently believe what we have decided to do or think is correct and not externally influenced. When external factors cause a direct change in our opinion and ideas without being identified we believe the source to be internal, giving it maximum credibility and strength. The most powerful example of this lies in groups. Groups that are notoriously difficult to get into or mandate a hazing to new recruits create a bond of membership that is exceptionally resilient.

Let's illustrate the power of the scarcity principle by looking at an extremely simple experiment. In 1975 researchers Adewole and Worchel Lee tested the scarcity principlexxiii using two identical glass jars and some cookies. Their purpose was to see how the amount of cookies available influenced perception of value. One jar held ten cookies while the other held only two. Which one do you think was perceived as more desirable? The jar with only two was substantially more favorable.

In another experiment that is search-able on YouTube, researchers tested the effect of context within the realm of the scarcity principle. World-class violinist Joshua Bell played a free impromptu concert in a Washington, DC subway hall. Bell, one of the best violinists in the world, regularly sells out huge concert halls charging hundreds of dollars per ticket. However, context truly is king; no one paid any attention to Joshua while he played in the subway station. This is a powerful lesson in marketing; when something special is available for free it becomes unappreciated and unnoticed. This is actually the logic behind higher prices on information products, not only can companies generate higher revenues but people believing the price to be an indicator of scarcity will actually apply themselves to learn and use the information they have paid for.

Perhaps the scarcity principle is best thought of in terms of a graph. As the perceived scarcity of an object rises, the desire to own it and its inherent value increases.

Conversely, as the abundance of an item increases the perceived value or desire to own it actually dissipates. The jar with only two cookies was too attractive to resist. However, when that number increased to ten, the cookies weren't valued as much. Scarcity is a powerful evolutionary based principle that can easily affect our perception. Just remember that the next time you go to grab the last slice of pizza.

Halo Effect: When You Are so Beautiful People Can't Say No

Eric and Bob have applied for the same job. Despite Bob having slightly better qualifications for the job, Eric is chosen over him. The decision was a tough one for the human resources people in charge of hiring. They weren't sure who to pick but eventually chose Eric as he seemed more reliable and more confident.

Psychologist Edward Thorndike first used this term "halo" to refer to a person who is perceived as having a halo that influences all related perceptions. The halo bias is actually a cognitive bias (mental shortcut in thinking) in which a person's impression of a person, brand, or company influences every other aspect. A poignant example is a beautiful person. Beautiful people are given preferential treatment and reserved a sense of respect that is based solely on their looks. The "halo" of beauty forms the impression by which we make all other assumptions about a person's character, ability and competence. Our impression of beauty makes us more likely to be convinced someone is more intelligent, more knowledgeable and more trustworthy. Even if we don't know it, we are greatly affected by beautiful people. They are powerful symbols of status and worth in our brains. For this reason, the halo effect of beauty is a powerful form of social compliance and persuasion.

The term "halo" is an analogy originated from a religious concept. Medieval and Renaissance paintings often include a glowing circle that can be seen floating above the heads of various saints. The glowing light of the halo indicates a person favored by God or possessing virtues of high worth. The observer, upon seeing the halo, now sees this character as a saintly figure. Our judgment is transferred from one object to all characteristics of a person's character.

In 1972, a studyxxiv conducted on the relationship between attractiveness and the halo effect demonstrated the power of this form of persuasion. Sixty students from the University of Minnesota participated in the experiment—half male and half female. Subjects were given three photographs to examine and then rate: one of an attractive individual, one of an average individual, and one of an unattractive individual. Subjects were also asked to assess twenty-seven personality traits including kindness, sexual promiscuity, emotionality, trustworthiness and altruism. The final assessment called for students to rate the predicted happiness and success of the person in the photo. Were they likely to get divorced? Have a great job? Have great parents? What status was their job?

So before we continue on, what do you think you would do? Would you rate people equally or would your answers reveal a hidden bias towards the beautiful? Unsurprisingly, results showed that people were overwhelmingly convinced that attractive subjects were better on almost all fronts. On every measurement the sixty students rated attractive people as more competent, more successful and more likable. In case you hadn't noticed yet, us humans are a pretty superficial bunch.

We have just learned to hide our superficiality but our mental shortcuts make us disposed to view beauty as a sign of good genes. This is what beauty is about. Let's face the truth of the matter. Beauty in nature indicates superior genes; superior genes indicate better health for potential offspring. Unfortunately, the extent of the beauty bias extends its corrupting tentacles even deeper into human society.

A study of a 1974xxv Canadian federal election showed that attractive candidates received more than two and a half times more votes than unattractive candidates. With several historical examples aside we are biased toward good-looking leaders even when we deny it. Despite the preference shown for attractive political candidates, follow-up research showed that voters didn't even realize their bias. Naturally, the workplace isn't safe from this bias either. You might not be surprised to know that attractive, well-groomed people get hired in interviews much more often than unattractive people—despite the fact that employers claim that appearance didn't play a part in the decision process. However, what is surprising is that the advantage extends itself to payday too. Yes, being beautiful means you get paid more. Economists examining U.S. and Canadian samples concluded that attractive individuals get paid an average of 12-14 percent more than their unattractive coworkers. So the next time you decide to skip shaving your beard or cutting your hair that looks like a family of birds nested inside of it, think about this.

What about the law? Can a person look guilty? Can you look at an individual and just decide—based on his crooked nose, hunched back, perpetual scowl and bad teeth—that he is the perpetrator of the crime? If you start to get that, I just know it was him, feeling then you should know attractive individuals get better treatment and smaller sentences. A 1990 study xxvi by Downs and Lyon revealed that individuals with good body and bone structures (I would love to know how they evaluated bone structure) are likely to receive highly favorable sentences. Researchers rated the physical attractiveness of 74 male defendants at the start of criminal trials. After subsequent sentencing, results showed that handsome men received significantly lighter sentences. This wasn't by a small margin either—in fact, attractive defendants were twice as likely to avoid jail as unattractive people. In cases involving money, ugly people got an average of 5,623 in compensation whereas the attractive ones got 10,050. Now, this doesn't mean if you look like Brad Pitt you should go out committing a crime thinking, I'm too handsome to be convicted, but it does demonstrate the subtle yet powerful influence of beauty.

Perhaps one of the factors that make beauty so convincing is that to admit it influenced you makes you look incredibly superficial. Sure, we all have a superficial side to us, but part of the game of life is to hide that superficiality under a series of stories and fabricated lies. We don't like to be exposed for the mental shortcutting homo sapiens we are.

Similarity: When You Like Things That Are Similar

Tom: Hey, I love that shirt. Is that a Chicago Cubs shirt?

Eric: Sure is.

Tom: My best friend is from Chicago. I was up there last June and went to a Cubs game. It was a great time.

We like people who are interested in us. Being friendly and showing others that you like them is a very overlooked form of persuasion. This is generally stereotyped as "sucking up" and is viewed quite negatively, but when done subtly and not so blatantly it works well. Telling someone how good he or she is or how well they are doing something can sometimes appear too obvious. However, if done in a subtle way it usually flies under the radar and produces the same feelings of endearment.

We like those who are similar to us; this similarity can be shared in any number of ways. From place of birth to past hobbies, demonstrating similarity for another immediately primes them to start liking you. This liking is based on trust. A base level of trust is extended towards people who have a similar geographic, personal or professional bond. We act as if they are one of the tribe and with that membership also comes a reciprocal relationship to help other tribe members out. In a world of anonymity similarity brings people together. This is especially potent if you are far away from home and meet someone from the same country or even the same city. The bond between similar people tightens and helping them is like helping ourselves. Our entire process of initial introductions and greetings is based off the idea of trust building.

We greet someone, smile, shake hands and then ask them about their family or health. This entire process builds up to the point where we can effectively say, "I care about you and like you. I want to know what is happening in your life. Please trust me." Demonstrating similarity while using a few "I like ___" compliments encourages others to feel that you genuinely care about them. This can be further exaggerated if you remember a particular detail about them from a previous conversation or interaction.

Similarity is so powerful that even when we encounter people who hold different opinions than us we still comply with their requests. In a study by Paul Silvia participants xxvii were given two sets of essays that threatened subjects' attitudinal freedom (the essay was contrary to a view that the participants held). The first essay's author shared the same name as the participants, and an identical birthday, however the second author did not. Despite being the same essays, only participants who read the article where the author's name and birthday were the same as theirs reported a strong sense of support and agreement. Those individuals who believed that they shared a similarity with the author also tended to believe more strongly that the author shared similar personal values with themselves, compared to individuals who did not believe they had a similarity with the author. This has also been shown via social media. When contacted by a stranger who shared two similar interests (not group membership) people were more than four times as likely to accept the friend request.

This tendency for similarity to increase the degree of liking also appears when the similarities are more personal. In a study by Insko and Wilson xxviii , participants who perceived sharing similar personalities with another individual tended to rate this individual higher on a likability scale, compared to those participants who perceived sharing dissimilar personalities with the other individual. Liking people with similar personalities isn't overly surprising but the extent of similarity bias is shocking. In one study on this phenomenon, individuals were shown to be significantly more attracted to people whose last names shared letters with their own, as well as people whose meaningless experimental code numbers were associated with their birthday numbers. The tendency not only affects seemingly subjective and fickle attractions, but also major life decisions, such as city of residence, spouse, and career.

The subtle nature of similarity makes it an effective tool of social compliance. In a study by Guéguenxxix, participants complied more often and more quickly to a request for completing an online survey sent via e-mail from a solicitor of the same surname than of a differing surname. The next time you are in a position where you want to befriend someone or gain another person's favor know that making yourself appear similar to them creates an instant bond. The principle of ingratiation is more about liking than anything. It is about trust.

Association: When We Like People Who Are Associated with Good Things

Exotic car shows involve three things: Cars you can't afford, women dressed provocatively, and hordes of gawking onlookers.

Ideas don't exist independently in our minds. Instead they function in an interconnected web of meaning similar to the actual physical structure of our brains. We connect mental things together and the outcome of those connections is associations—the associations of pairing two stimuli together. If repeated often enough, this becomes the standard that all future impressions are based on. By connecting yourself or your idea to another idea, the resulting association can serve to persuade.

The most common application of this association is with beauty. Advertisers have long accepted the idea that "beauty sells" and have utilized attractive celebrity endorsers, spokespeople, and models in their advertisements. Empirical studies demonstrate this phenomenon, showing that physical attractiveness of a person shown in an ad increases advertiser credibility, willingness to purchase, direct mail response rate, attitude towards the product, and actual purchase. Furthermore, this effect is found when both male and female models are used in print advertising, point of purchase displays, actual communicators in one-on-one interactions, and for celebrity endorsements. Beyond physical appearance, associating character and personality with products can be an effective method of persuasion. We see this often in advertising where corporate sponsors attempt to align their products with professional athletes.

Some of these associations are extreme. Who would have thought that McDonald's would be the official sponsor of the Olympics?

Associations provide handy shortcuts for thinking. These quick assumptions are what you first think of when you see a product. This same works for people's association with a certain idea, it will be remembered specifically for that. This is best demonstrated by advertising. What do you think of when you hear the names of various car companies? Toyota – reliable. BMW – expensive. Jeep – strong. These concepts come to our mind the second we come in contact with the idea. When these associations with items are paired with powerful emotions, the strength and resiliency of that association is even stronger. Meeting someone for the first time and experiencing a powerful emotional event can tie you to that person, the associations between the emotions experienced and the person can create a powerful bond that lasts. The first impression is the most critical when creating association. This is also known as the "anchoring effect"; like a ship's anchor we overly value the first piece of information we experience, essentially weighing down all subsequent information.

The power of association can also be seen in the use of pronouns and sports teams. We want to be associated with positive events and outcomes not negative ones. People will be quick to claim association with a successful outcome much more readily than a negative one. This is exemplary of our inner need to be seen as good. Allowing another person to associate what they have done or think about themselves with something positive fulfills this function. The next time you're talking with a group of people about a problem that everyone is experiencing, pay attention to the use of pronouns, specifically the usage of "we/us" as opposed to "you/they". The decision to associate yourself or create separation demonstrates our need for positive associations. When our favorite sports team wins we say, "We did it," however when they lose it becomes, "They should have..." The same goes for office/social politics, assigning "we" and "they" create the powerful first impressions we talked about earlier. The ability to assign blame fulfills an essential need in our minds—the need for a just and orderly world. By associating others or ourselves with success or loss we create reasons for why events were successful or unsuccessful.

So the next time you are interacting with someone think about the medium in which you are together. Is it an emotionally arousing situation? What are you associating your argument or yourself with?

Exclusivity: When You Feel Special

We normally offer a 5% discount on that product but if you join our limited-time membership I can see if it's possible to get you the 20% exclusive members-only purchase.

We like to feel special or that we have special privileges. Knowing that we have met the "qualifications or qualities" to get a special favor or piece of information can make us much more willing to comply with a request. Remember how we talked about reactance earlier? Exclusivity works on a similar fundamental. In reactance, when we are told we cannot have something our sense of control is offended and so we are motivated to take control. Similarly, when we know that we qualify for something our sense of identity is boosted and there is a sense of confidence gained by knowing that we belong to a "special group".

Exclusivity can also come in the form of secret information that isn't otherwise given. I'm sure we have all experienced savvy marketers who attempt to entice us to sign up with promises of sharing otherwise undistributed information. When presenting an offer, or "framing", the exclusivity principle should be used to full effect for maximum persuasive value. In a 1982, researcher named Amran Knishinsky xxx documented an excellent example. He studied the purchase decisions of wholesale beef buyers. He observed that they more than doubled their orders when they were told that, because of certain weather conditions overseas, there was likely to be a scarcity of foreign beef in the near future. But their orders increased 600% when they were informed that no one else had that information yet. Scarcity increased the orders but when you combine scarcity with exclusivity you get a recipe for powerful persuasion.

The driving force behind this is the same feeling you get when a friend mentions a secret that he or she wants to tell you later or some special news. The anticipation is almost too much to handle and we become anxious to hear what it is. This is a more innocuous version of the stock market "hot tip". Many investors have lost their life savings or purchased funds and stocks that they otherwise wouldn't have, all based on the idea of an exclusive hot tip. A recent example of this comes to mind; a coworker's wife works at a large bank's investment office that deals primarily with currency exchange. She told me that, two weeks prior; several upper-level employees lost an outrageous sum of money betting on commodities—all based on hot tips received via the security guard at the front gate. Now, this is an extreme example but nonetheless still a valid example of how informational exclusivity or the perception of it can quickly circumnavigate logic.

We all have a vital need for esteem and for a sense of identity; allowing another person to share with you an experience or product that is exclusive and not easily accessible to everyone else forms the basis of this tool of persuasion. Why do you think expensive brands do so well? Their price tags exemplify a form of exclusivity excluding the average person from purchasing. Aligning ourselves with an item or idea that is only accessible to a few fulfills our need to be seen as special and unique amongst a sea of other people.

Consistency: When You Make Commitments about Yourself

Seller: So you said your price range is 15,000? Correct?

Buyer: Yes, around that.

Seller: O.K., I'll try to find you that model for that price. If I find it will you buy one today?

Buyer: Well. We will see, but I think I will.

The world is a crazy place. We crave predictability and when it doesn't exist we create it. We want to see ourselves as predictable, as people with fixed personality and character traits that allow us to say, "I am kind, I am helpful." We establish standards for ourselves and self-regulate behavior to comply with those standards. We talked about this earlier in self-perception theory; the idea that behavior that doesn't conform to our self-expectations creates cognitive dissonance. This is where the power of consistency lies, by making affirmations about who we are or what we will do in the future we create a powerful need to conform to that affirmation in order to appear consistent. We must align our actions and promises with our inner choices and belief systems. Failure to do so will result in lowered self-esteem.

The power of persuasion rests dangerously in this ability to get people to make affirmations. Consistency works on two levels. First, you feel compelled to comply with the affirmation and, second, you feel that the need was created internally not externally. We internalize the goal as one that truly originated from ourselves and was not spurred by some outward encouragement. We may even feel we have a

68

free choice, which, in some sense, we do. If we were unlike most people we could simply go back on our affirmations and break the bond of consistency but we usually don't. From the time we were young our mothers told us to keep our word and not lie, so instead we believe we have made a free choice and feel personally responsible to carry through and justify it. I know this may sound like brainwashing; that is because it is. Yes, brainwashing works exactly the same. The key to brainwashing is to use small, incremental actions that increasingly demonstrate each new belief. Each step may seem inconsequential, but slowly the beliefs change internally in order to justify what is happening externally. These small requests eventually transition up to bigger ones. This incorporates some of the earlier persuasion methods we talked about, namely the foot in the door technique (asking for something small first).

Let's look at one of the most powerful examples of this slow, step-by-step, incremental, increasing consistency principle. During the Korean War Chinese communists held many American POWs; upon their return home they received extensive medical and psychiatric evaluation. Results showed that a great majority of them held pro-communist beliefs and some outright supported the communist agenda. This phenomenon was unheard of; POW camps were generally miserable, terrible places where brutality and inhumanity was the rule of law. The POWs extolled the virtues of their captors and what they had learned. This sparked a studyxxxi into what had happened. It was concluded that, "Prisoners were frequently asked to make statements so mildly anti-American or pro-Communist as to seem inconsequential (e.g. 'The United States is not perfect.'). But once these minor requests were complied with, the men found themselves pushed to submit to related, yet more substantive requests."

Commitments included keeping a journal, writing letters to family and friends, making public speeches or discussing publically the values of the communist system. These men were also given rewards for exhibiting the appropriate pro-communist behavior. This experiment is of huge importance. It showed that affirmations and can modify behavior to a massive extent. Soldiers who had been risking their lives fighting communism became communist sympathizers. This form of persuasion is best utilized in active public forums. This form of groupthink played a powerful role. Perhaps the most insidious element of the Chinese brainwashing was asking Americans to sign every document that they had authored. The physical act of signing something united the prisoner with the ideas he had identified with.

Let's look at this in a closer context. In 1983 Israeli researchers xxxii asked half the residents of a large apartment complex to sign a petition to establish a new handicapped recreation center. The request was small and the cause was good so the majority of requestees signed the petition. Two weeks later, on National Collection Day for the Handicapped, all the residents of the complex were approached and asked to donate. Over half of the people who had not signed a petition agreed to give money. This paled in comparison to the amazing ninety-two percent of people who had previously signed the petition and donated. Signing the petition earlier had made them aligned with the idea of helping build a new recreation area and when the time came they needed to live up to their commitments. Again we see that public commitments are the most powerful.

To create truly difficult to break consistency, social compliance experts seek to get people to make statements or omissions that can't be easily gone back on and are displayed in a social forum. Written statements are the most powerful. In an experiment described in a 1955 issue of the Journal of Abnormal Psychology xxxiii, college students were asked to estimate the length of lines projected onto a screen. Students were asked to write down their choices, sign it and give it to the researcher. In another group students were asked to write it on an erasable piece of whiteboard and the final group were told to just keep the answer to themselves. The students who had just remembered the answer by themselves were the fastest to reconsider their original estimates. The ones who had signed the document and handed it to the researcher almost never changed their estimate in the many trials conducted. The lesson is clear. Be wary of documents asking for permission or agreement. Once we make a public statement it's hard to recant. Read the fine print.

This brings me to my last point about the principle of consistency—commitments that are voluntary are the most powerful. An external pressure forcing someone to make a commitment can backfire terribly. We talked earlier of the tendency for reactance. Pressure to commit to an idea that we don't value is a recipe for supercharged reactance. A true wizard of social compliance goes about it in a different way. Identifying what another person values greatly and then describing how a certain action is a great example of those values creates an internal need to modify one's behavior. This occurs because we want to conform to others' positive expectations of us, failure to do so would mean we aren't as competent or good as they view us. As we adopt the values and actions they are extolling, we take ownership of that consistency belief and pave the path for true persuasion. We believe the decision to commit to this new belief; value or action was our own.

Amplification/Attentuation: When You Make Little Things Bigger and Make Bigger Things Smaller

Person A: Did you hear what happened to Cindy?

Person B: No. What happened? I haven't heard anything!

Person A: She got robbed on her trip. She is lucky, she could have been killed. It's incredibly dangerous where she went. I absolutely can't believe she would go there. We all need to pay attention to safety. I know you agree; it's just so dangerous.

We can all think of some people who exaggerate in every situation. These hyperbolic distorters of facts make things bigger or more significant than they actually are. This significance or seeming importance arouses both our biology and our attention. A general technique or rhetoric is guiding people toward points that support our ideas and away from those that reduce our argument. We amplify the points we support and downgrade those we don't. However, there is a lot of room within this subtle space. Each of these individual points can be made more dramatic by pointing out potential dangers or rewards. Let's use the above conversation as an example and break down each point of amplification.

- In this case, pointing out another person's need for safety and acknowledging their agreement with that statement helps amplify it.

- Contrasting the consequences of not following along with that piece of action are also implied—if you travel there is danger.

- Using emotionally loaded language to stress key words and make them stand out.

- Repeating messages to reemphasize the points already made.

- Asking for confirmation of an idea based on another person's actions.

- Expanding the truth to imply next-in-line events could have and probably will come true.

- Framing small things as bigger than they actually were (perhaps the robbery was just a watch left unattended).

You can see that all of these fit together to create an amplified story that sends your mind spinning into the possibility of disaster. Our future predictions become tainted by the subtle techniques of amplification. However, exaggeration also works in the opposite way by downgrading and downplaying the facts, opinions and potentials. Let's look at this conversation.

Person A: Do you think we should tell the boss about our failed project? He might find out.

Person B: It's not important, plus you didn't even spend much time on the project so it's not your issue. It's a non-issue. If you go and tell what happened he might get angry, I don't want that to happen. We don't have to bother him with every little detail. Also, you know I've handled this kind of thing before.

This is the process of attenuating or downplaying an argument or point to persuade someone. Let's look at what is happening here.

- Distracting the person away from the point in question, notifying him or her that it isn't important.

- Decreasing an individual's investment in an action to make them feel that they aren't responsible or in control.

- Reframing the point or issue in question to reestablish how it is perceived. In this case, person B says, "It's a non-issue."

- Hurting the person and providing alternatives for that pain. This often starts with statements that warn of the future possibility for unpleasantness.

- Trivializing items that might be used against the argument or trivializing the point in general.

- Framing yourself as an authority figure who can be trusted to carry out or handle this task.

Just as you would adjust an amplifier you can turn up and turn down the power of different points to achieve whatever persuasive point you want to achieve. This ensures recipients only receive a series of biased choices. When you don't have access to all the information possible, sometimes asking for personal advice is asking for biased advice. The information that is conveyed is not objectively delivered to you for your consideration but rather passes a subjective filter, which taints the ideas and opinions towards those of the presenter. It is a form of managed truth and we use it constantly. You might think this seems immoral or somehow dishonest, but, if you can, notice yourself doing it constantly. We don't see it as deliberate lying but instead as an economic manipulation of different facts. We stretch the truth or compact its importance by utilizing contrasting elements. We make things bigger by reducing those around it and vice versa.

This method of persuasion is very subtle. It involves a tuning up or down of the various frequencies of points and their relative strength and frequency. Be wary of any person actively extolling the virtues of one item while attenuating another. Doing your own research is the best way to avoid this.

Danger and Rescue: When You Feel Frightened and Look for Safety

That doesn't sound like a great idea, Eric. Changing careers so suddenly is a risky idea. What if it doesn't work well? What about the pension you have been working on building? What if you hate it?

When we come into contact with a situation or event that is deemed dangerous, logic isn't our first response. Our natural response is that of fight-or-flight, a biological remnant of our prehistoric past. Warning others of associated dangers can bypass the rational consideration and lead them directly into a state of social compliance in the form of "safety". This safety is provided by the persuader to provide sanctuary from a danger that he invented or exaggerated. This danger doesn't come in the form of a large predatory animal but instead within suggestions of the possibility of embarrassment, failure, social alienation, grief, guilt or regret. If exaggerated through some of the principles we talked about in the previous session, we have an effective recipe for making people uncomfortable enough to seek immediate remedy.

What I am talking about is a threat hidden within the context of a suggestion, idea or opinion. Threats attack deep needs—needs for safety, esteem, respect and health. When our fundamental needs are in jeopardy we forget our higher aspirations and quickly work to find a way to protect ourselves. One of the most powerful threats is the loss of autonomy; the idea of losing control is almost unbearable to most of us.

These threats produce tension. Tension is the driving force

behind all manner of persuasive techniques but in this case the tension produced is more overtly felt. This tension is felt throughout the body and yearns for a release. We seek a release from this tension and an opposing pull back and forth on the two can sometimes be too much to bear. Think of the idea of "good cop bad cop". This is a game of opposites of tension and kindness and it makes weaker people fold. Tension can be pulled back and forth by precise words or suggestions. Suggesting that a person has not lived up to their values can create an internal tension state as they attempt to align their actions with their value systems.

Tension can also be created effectively through uncertainty. Uncertainty defies our need for control and certainty, when we are unsure about the future we cannot accurately predict what will happen. We begin to feel the associated tension of uncertainty. This makes us more willing to seek information or ideas that will bring resolution.

Tension can also come in the form of excitement. When we are excited to the point of anxiousness it can be pleasantly uncomfortable and there is an immediate relief in getting the overly stimulating action completed. For me this is best explained by a roller coaster ride. The anxiety and fear you feel through every twist and turn eventually culminates in a nervous release as the car stops and you jump out to immediately share how you felt with your friends.

The safety method can work in two different ways and both can be used to persuade ruthlessly. If we concentrate on a desirable future then we will be pulled towards it as we hope to achieve that future result. For example, "If you follow my advice you will receive ten thousand dollars and be happy." The second method of providing safety is when we focus first on the undesirable event; we want to move away from it or avoid it. In each situation social compliance can be reached effectively. However, there is a third option, which is known as "satisficing", a combination of satisfying and sufficing. In this situation we just grab whatever option is provided to us in a desperate need to end the tension.

So the next time someone is insistent on mentioning the dangers associated with an event, be careful when they offer a solution in their favor. Consider whether the decision you are about to make is based on an emotional state they have created or your own free, rational decision.

Social Proof: When You Look to Others for What to Do

If you were walking down the street and saw two or three people looking up at the sky would you stop and look or just keep on walking?

A famous quote says, "You are the sum total of the five people you spent the most time with." This is an example of the phenomenon of social proof. We use others as a metric for what actions we should or shouldn't engage in. We look for the correct behavior in a given situation or time and follow it. This habit is displayed more commonly in ambiguous social situations where we lack understanding of how to socially function. The reasoning behind social proof is simple—it's a mental shortcut. Mental shortcuts are also known as heuristics. Heuristics originate from the Greek word for "find" and they are rules of thumb we utilize to quickly and efficiently categorize a situation or person. They are those first assumptions that we use to navigate the world quickly.

Social proof is also commonly displayed in what is referred to as heard behavior, where the sheer force of numbers dilutes the choices of individuals. You may be wondering why social proof is the last form of persuasion, as it's not directly applied by one person but rather a group of people. The answer lies in the power of social proof—understanding how social proof functions gives you a valuable insight into any socially based persuasive methods. The more people who are doing it the more careful you need to be. Social proof is a form of conformity; it leads not only to public compliance but also private compliance. It is often coupled with authority to produce a more powerful effect.

In one of the most famous experiments conducted by Muzafer Sherifxxxiv in 1935 subjects were placed into a dark room and asked to observe a dot of light located 15 meters away. They were asked how much the light was moving. In reality, the light was not moving but only appeared to be moving. The variation in different subjects' estimates was standard and generally consistent over time for each new person. Several days later the second part of the experiment took place. This time subjects were paired with two other subjects and asked to give the same estimate on how much the light was moving—but this time they had to say it aloud. Despite the fact that subjects had given totally different estimates previously they would come to a common estimate. To avoid the potential that subjects were giving a different answer just to satisfy the group needs, researchers had subjects re-judge the light again without the group. Results showed that they still maintained the group's judgment. Sherif concluded that, since the stimulus was ambiguous, the participants were relying on each other to define reality.

When individuals are placed in a social environment their ability to independently make decisions and adhere to those decisions falls under the influential sway of the group dynamic. The influence of social proof is subtle and may not be obvious immediately. Like some of the other forms of persuasion we discussed earlier, the most powerful overall changes are implemented on a small basis. Small concessions lead to big outcomes.

Another example of subtle influence comes to us from the

Asch Conformity Experiments. In 1951, researcher Solomon Aschxxxv conducted an experiment that laid the groundwork for a long line of conformity studies. Subjects were given a piece of paper with three horizontal lines drawn on it. The lines were of equal thickness and uniformity, however one was longer. Students were asked to individually decide which one was longer. Then they conducted this experiment again with three other confederates (scientists disguised as people) who purposely selected the wrong lines. Despite clearly seeing which line was the longest, subjects still sided with the group opinion and chose the incorrect line. Simply being outnumbered in opinion makes it much easier to succumb to this social proof bias and be persuaded into changing your opinion.

What if the situation didn't involve a simple line but instead a person's guilt or innocence? Another experiment looked at social proof in eyewitness identification. Subjects were shown a picture of a "perpetrator"; they were then shown pictures of four other men and asked to pick out the one they had just seen. However, the subject was not alone; in the room were three other confederates who all selected the wrong person. Subjects were then asked to make a selection of the perpetrator based on two scenarios: first, that they were participating in a real test of eyewitness identification ability that would be used in court or, second, that the task wasn't so serious and they were just looking for hints to improve the task. Results showed that subjects who thought the task was of high importance conformed 51 % of the time, selecting the wrong person. This is in contrast to the 35% who conformed via the lower pressure condition.

The two experiments above describe the effects of social proof but also another alarming feature of it—the suspension of our cognitive faculties. Not only are our judgments subject to peer influence but our responsibility for making those judgments is diminished. This is referred to as a "diffusion of responsibility", the idea that the more people surround you the less you feel responsible to act. There is a pause and a delay where we think to ourselves, Should I do something? I'm sure someone else is in charge or will take care of it. Within this delay the responsibility of individual action is attenuated to the point where we may just stand idly by. This can have small implications or terrifying implications. Let's use a more powerful example to illustrate this effect.

In the 1970s a horrific murder took place, that of Kitty Genovese. The young woman was horribly beaten and stabbed for over half an hour in a public display of barbarity. Over forty residents in nearby buildings witnessed and heard the entire ordeal but no one called for the police. Kitty eventually died as onlookers watched and listened. When others are present we assume that they will take action or look to others to see what actions they should take. In this case, the residents, who were not particularly cruel or inhumane people, simply felt that their neighbors had surely called the police and they themselves wouldn't have to. The responsibility of being a good person was diffused amongst a group of people through the assumption that they would act.

This lack of action and paralysis in emergency situations has been widely documented and researchers have shown there is one extremely effective way to curtail it—give specific orders to specific people. Yelling and pointing to another person and telling them, "You in the grey shirt, call the police right now," is much more effective than just waiting for them to hopefully contact the police or ambulance.

If you look around you can see examples of social proof in every facet of life. In a world filled with so much noise and information it can be taxing to make rational decisions for everything. By following what others do we are given a path of safety in which to navigate social interactions. Not only do we follow but sometimes the examples demonstrated by others allow us to carry out acts that we otherwise wouldn't partake in. If I told you that suicide and homicide rates increase after media reports of such events would you believe me? This phenomenon, known as "copycat suicide", shows that when similarities are perceived between the person publicized and the potential copycat the likelihood of a similar act occurring is much higher. The death of Marilyn Monroe alone increased suicide rates the following month by over two hundredxxxvi.

Social proof is not some malicious flaw in our society. It isn't designed to cause us to make irrational choices and damage our lives. The negative effects of it are often emphasized and researched because they are the more quantifiable and memorable ones. This makes it easy to forget that social proof is a mental shortcut that allows us to make decisions quickly and effectively. While we may study where social proof went wrong, the innumerable benefits that it provides can't be measured. Following others without thought can blind you into conforming to ideas and opinions you wouldn't generally subscribe to, but it also serves to simplify reality and decisions.

Our 25 Persuasive Techniques

In the next chapter I will give you twenty-four sample situations and ask you to identify which forms of persuasion were used. Before we begin we must review what we have learned thus far:

1. Foot In The Door

A method of compliance that involves making a small request first followed by a sequence of increasingly bigger requests. When people comply with the first request they are more likely to acquiesce to the second as they see themselves as cooperative and helpful.

2. Bait and Switch

When one product or idea is offered to secure a person's interest. Once interest is garnered and the person commits to some form of action the initial item is switched for another in its stead.

3. Door In The Face

A ridiculously large request is initially made; this is then followed up by a request that seems much smaller in comparison. This utilizes the law of contrast to make people more likely to comply.

4. Lowball

This method of persuasion involves an item or service being offered at lower price than is actually intended. After a customer has expressed interest in purchasing and made a verbal commitment to that interest, the price is raised to increase profits on the initially cheaply advertised product. This can work with an idea or suggestion, too, when it is advertised as more convenient or better than it actually is.

5. Closure Principles

The closure principle works on the basis of tension creation. An incredible amount of tension is created to the point where someone seeks resolution. The resolution a person seeks is often the goal or objective of the person using this method of persuasion.

6. Authority Principle

We abjectly convey knowledge, power and intelligence to any symbols of authority. We have an innate tendency to coalesce to such forms of authority and do as they command us. Utilizing authority or adopting its symbols can serve to persuade extremely effectively.

7. Clothing

Following the law of authority, clothing is one of the most potent symbols of authority. For example, wearing a lab coat or a business suit conveys a superior sense of knowledge and intelligence more so than just wearing regular clothing.

8. Reactance

When the perception of our personal freedoms is threatened we react immediately, often attempting to move against the initial reaction to protect ourselves. This is the need to rebel against control.

9. Altruism

Appealing to people's need to be helpful, considerate and kind is the appeal to altruism. "Since you are a good person I know you will help me."

10. Negative Self Feeling

If you don't help another person you will feel bad. The threat of potential negative feelings of guilt, sadness, anger or regret can persuade people into compliance.

11. Pleading

Pleading is just begging. Begging lowers your social status and raises another person's, making them more likely to help you. It isn't the most desirable method of persuasion but it works well. Acting like a child or using childlike begging techniques can also achieve this.

12. Ingratiation

Making another person like you is a powerful method to make them willing to help you. Gifts, flattery and association can achieve this.

13. **Reciprocity**

Whether you know it or not, receiving gifts makes us want to reciprocate. Even if we don't want the gift we still feel obliged to return the favor. There is often an overcompensation that occurs where the returned gift is of larger worth or value than the initially received gift.

14. **Framing**

The way you position yourself and the kind of information that you surround your idea or suggestion with influences how others perceive it. Ideas are not considered alone but rather within a framework of circumstances, emotion and past history.

15. **Inferences**

Following along with the idea of framing, when an idea is

explained but certain key details are omitted, others are forced to make assumptions. If the persuader is skilled at explaining or framing a situation in a way that he or she wants then the logical inferences that others make may be biased.

16. Halo Effect

We ascribe positive attributes of confidence, intelligence and better abilities to people who are beautiful. This association is mostly unconscious.

17. Similarity

People who are similar to us in any way are more likable than those who aren't. This similarity can come from a variety of factors: background, education, family, political orientation or interests.

18. Association

People or events that are associated with positive stimulus are remembered better and more favorably. A person attempting to persuade you may connect his or her idea with a positive event to create that mental association.

19. Exclusivity

When access to anyone is restricted, the principles of competition and exclusivity create a powerful incentive to possess the item now. This incentive may override logic and cause a person to want an item much more than before.

20. Consistency

When you make an affirmation or a promise you experience a powerful need to remain consistent with that promise. A good persuader can talk you into making those affirmations, which serve to modify your future behavior to comply and remain consistent.

21. **Amplification/Attenuation**

Similar to framing, this is the tuning up and down of ideas, feelings or informational salience to exaggerate certain points and downplay others.

22. **Danger and rescue**

When threat is emphasized to the point that the other feels frightened about a potential event a powerful sense of tension is created. Similar to the closure principle, this tension seeks resolution, which the persuader luckily has prepared.

23. **Social proof**

We use others as a metric for what activities we should engage in. This is a heuristic, a mental shortcut that allows us to make decisions faster and more effectively. Utilizing social proof is a powerful persuasion technique.

Guess the Persuasion Technique

Now that we have learned and studied how each method affects us, we will look at some sample conversations and decide which one of these persuasion techniques each person is utilizing. Keep in mind that more than one may be used in each example. Below is a series of conversations where you must assign the correct persuasion technique to each method. At the bottom you will find a short explanation of the answer—please avoid looking at the answer before reading the conversation.

Bob: I can't believe you would take that medicine! You know how unhealthy it is. My friend Susan took it last month and she developed a benign tumor that had to be surgically removed!

Sally: Oh my God! Not Susan! She is so nice, what did she do? I don't want that to happen to me.

Bob: She is O.K. now, but it was pretty scary. I have a better idea, why don't you buy some of this herbal supplement with me? It works better and, best of all, it's totally safe.

Sally: O.K. That sounds good. Thanks so much, how much is it?

Person A is making mention of tumors and, by extension, threatening person B. The danger that is implied creates tension, which is where Bob gracefully introduces his offer to purchase a herbal remedy with him. This is the Danger and Rescue principle.

Bob: Hey, are you going to that new electronics store? They ship directly from the factory so they have great deals.

Sally: No. I haven't heard about it.

Bob: Well, they are only open for another week or so and most of their products have already been purchased. They have a really limited supply.

Sally: Where is it? I'll stop by after work.

The exclusivity that is created by mentioning competition and limited time conveys a sense of exclusivity that is hard to avoid. Sally may have not wanted to go there before but she is definitely interested now. This is the principle of Exclusivity.

Bob is forced to select a new candidate for a job opening as a sales director. He carefully weighs his options and decides that the two best people for the job are Susan and Mary. The problem is their qualifications are identical as is their work experience. After a long period of consideration Bob chooses Mary who is much more attractive than Susan.

Although Bob may not know it, he is falling under the unconscious impression that Mary is somehow more confident and skilled than Susan. This is the halo effect. Research has shown that the impression of increased ability conferred by physical beauty often escapes conscious consideration and factors into our decision making process.

Whenever Susan visits her child's teacher she makes it a point to bring her a little token of her appreciation, whether it's a homemade pie or some cookies it doesn't matter. The teacher appreciates these gifts even though she doesn't particularly enjoy teaching Susan's child. Despite this the teacher often finds herself spending extra time and energy helping the child even when he has been naughty or disrespectful.

91

Receiving gifts, whether we want them or not, still makes us feel obliged to return the behavior. This is the biological imperative that makes sharing possible. We would not share as willingly if we knew others would not occasionally return our favors. This is the principle of reciprocity.

Bob: You know I can't thank you enough for helping me last time. That was so nice of you; you are such a nice person.

Sally: Don't mention it, I just wanted to help.

Bob: I couldn't have done it last time without your help. I was starting a new project today and I used the ideas that you taught me last time. I almost finished it but there were a few pieces I couldn't figure out.

Sally: Oh. Really? Well, let me take a look.

Instead of directly asking for something we cut a piece of the conversation out and allow the other person to fill it for us. Most of the time they will do this for us, and when they do, the responsibility involved in its commitment will be theirs. Bob wanted Sally's help but he didn't want to ask for it, instead he labeled her as a helping person and then indicated he couldn't complete it. Sally naturally made the inference that she need to help him. This is the principle of inference.

Andy has been working at Celltech for fifteen years and most of his time there has been enjoyable. Recently, new management decided to put a shocking amount of rules and regulations on every action and procedure. He feels frustrated under the heavy burden of conforming to every rule and regulation. Andy finds himself sitting in weekly meetings and not sharing anything. He has ideas that could increase efficiency and increase sales but instead he keeps his mouth closed and doesn't say a word.

This is reactance at its finest. When external forces restrict our freedoms we feel compelled to react to this threat. However, sometimes we are unable to react. In Andy's case his reactance was his unwillingness to help his company and share his ideas; instead, in an act of defiance, he chose silence. This is the principle of reactance and it's one of the most powerful forms of persuasion.

Sally recently received a job as a manager at a new biotech company. She is young but learning quickly. She immediately befriends an entry level assistant who works in a nearby department. The assistant spends her lunch hours with Sally, often admiring her for her experience and quick ascension up the company ladder. The assistant, upon hearing that Sally's favorite food is Mexican, shouts excitedly that Mexican is also her favorite food and she cannot go a week without eating it. The next day she brings Sally a bottle of her favorite hot sauce. Good friends or persuasion in practice?

This is the concept of ingratiation. It is based on three fundamentals: gifts, flattery and association. Gifts, whether we want them or not, activate the principle of reciprocity— the powerful need to return favors given to us. Flattery is the oldest tactic in the persuasion book and it works. Association creates a bond with another person through a shared interest, history or experience. The more profound the shared experience the stronger the bond.

Andy has started a new research project with two teammates. One of the more senior researchers, Larry, has been working hard to help Andy. Larry indicates that, due to his busy schedule, he is willing to help Andy but Andy must occasionally agree to accomplish small projects for the team. Andy agrees and every week Larry gives out a small number of tasks to Andy while often reminding him about his commitment. After several months, the scale of tasks that Larry is assigning is increasing rapidly. Often projects take several hours as opposed to several minutes. Andy soon feels overwhelmed by the amount of work but feels compelled not to reject Larry's requests.

This is the principle of consistency. Self-perception theory dictates that our values will decide our behaviors. If our behavior does not conform to our values we will experience negative feelings. Since Andy has made a verbal commitment to help Larry, his affirmation will regulate his behavior. In order to see himself as a consistent person who lives up to his word, he feels utterly compelled to continue in his actions. This result is often replicated quite terribly in abusive relationships. The invested time and energy sparks a perception of commitment, which makes the abused party unwilling to leave.

After watching a recent health report about the importance of regular omega-3 fat intake, you decide to buy some supplements. You go to the local store and eventually pick one out of the multitude of brands. When you return home your friend inquires as to why you chose this particular brand. You mention that it was doctor recommended.

Any symbol of authority, whether it be clothing, a title, a badge or a professional designation, will serve to confer immediate respect from others. We are conditioned from birth to respect authority and to comply with its will. As children this serves us well and we are generally kept safe by authority figures throughout our lives. However, clever social compliance experts will mask themselves and their ideas in the symbols and words of authority to create a powerful need to obey their commands.

At a recent meeting discussing a new tactic for their company's social media campaign, Andy found himself nervously twitching in his chair. He was a new employee and the meeting room was intimidating. It contained all the mid and high level managers, numbering over twenty people. Andy had worked on social media campaigns before and knew that the tactic they wanted to employ was ineffectual. When the presenter asked if there were any opinions, comments or objections, Andy nervously looked around the room, unable to find any sympathizers with his idea. He thought to himself, If only one other person says something I will too. Unfortunately, no one said a thing and Andy kept quiet. Was Andy just scared or was there a lack of support?

This is the principle of social proof. We use what others do as a metric for what activities we should engage in ourselves. This shortcut in thinking makes the world a lot simpler and easier to comprehend. In this case there was no social support and Andy felt paralyzed to comply with the rest of his coworkers and keep silent.

Primitive Processes for a Modern World

You are now equipped with a powerful arsenal of persuasion techniques. Although our journey through the land of social compliance was short, it provided an important insight into how we operate. Hopefully, some of the situations we described will serve as examples to increase your awareness in future situations. You may think you would never dream of using some of these techniques; however, this may be far from the truth. The principles of persuasion are used all around us and are built into our language. One of the biggest takeaways from this book should be the unique insight into our minds that examining persuasion gives you.

Persuasion is the social evolution of a biological process of mental shortcuts. The need to appraise information in a succinct, efficient way conditioned us to assess our world in the simplest ways possible. Like looking at a giant mess of dots on a wall, our brains disseminate a pattern and infuse that pattern with meaning and purpose. This pattern becomes an impression, which is arranged alongside similar impressions. These eventually come together to form the lens, which creates our reality. The patterns we see condition the behavior we engage in and a feedback loop is built, one that works independently and requires no awareness. Within these automatic processes we achieve our final end—that of simplifying the world into understandable patterns.

When we understand how this primitive automaticity is an essential part of understanding how our decision making is influenced, we can see how we often base decisions off incredibly small pieces of information. Often this information is limited, irrelevant or inaccurate, however it activates our mental patterns into making assumptions, judgments and terrible mistakes. These little bits of pieces of information are persuasion. The beautiful person, the symbol of authority, the huge initial request and the social proof provided by others—these little bits of information are the first tug on the lawnmower engine of automatic decision making. Unfortunately, we don't always have all the time in the world to consider every fact and detail and weigh the advantages and disadvantages, so we must rely on this primitive automaticity in decision-making.

In a world so frenzied, busy and stressful as ours, we all feel the effects of information overload. Never before have humans lived in a time when information was so readily available. With this comes a powerful contradiction. Despite the fact that we live in a time of endless information, we rely more heavily on these "instincts" to cope. We feel overwhelmed and overburdened. The paradox of choice demands that the more choices you are given the less free you feel. Our technology grows exponentially while humans struggle to keep up with the information explosion.

For the majority of mankind's history information has been difficult to acquire. Valid information was traditionally only accessible by a few, select people. It was considered sacred and cherished. Now information has increased to the point that simply staying up to date in one specific field would require a full-time commitment. The pressure required to absorb and process all the information related to one's profession or personal pursuits is stressful. The problem is that information is just that, *information*; it is not knowledge about oneself or life. As we drown in a sea of facts, numbers and Facebook updates, our brains become a little less sharp and, unfortunately, more prone to persuasion.

Ultimately, the final lesson of this book was to learn about different methods of persuasion; however, there is another. If you read this far I believe you are a keen mind and will be one of the few able to share the deeper lesson involved here. In an increasingly complicated world we face the reality of being unable to process, absorb and retain all the information available to us. The overwhelming richness of the outside world causes an analysis of paralysis, which we remedy by focusing on one singular piece of information. However, within this singular focus we are left open to be manipulated and persuaded by outside forces. These mental shortcuts are sacred but we must be aware of their powerful potential to create self-deception.

That is it.

I hope I persuaded you.

[i] Freedman, J.L. & Fraser, S.C. (1966). Compliance without pressure: The foot-in-the-door technique. *Journal of Personality and Social Psychology,* 4, 195-202.

[ii] Burger, J. M. (1999). The foot-in-the-door compliance procedure: A multiple-process analysis and review. *Personality and Social Psychology Review*, 3, 303-325

[iii] Guéguen, N., Meineri, S., Martin, A., & Grandjean, I. (2010, December 29). The combined effect of the foot-in-the-door technique and the "but you are free" technique: an evaluation on the selective sorting of household wastes. *Ecopsychology*, 2(4), 231–237.

[iv] Cialdini, R. B., & Trost, M. R., (1998) Social influence: Social norms, conformity, and compliance. In D. T. Gilbert and S. T.Fiske (Eds.), The *Handbook of Social Psychology: Vol. 2.* (4th ed., pp. 151-192). Boston: Mcgraw-Hill.

[v] Cialdini, R. B., & Trost, M. R., (1998) Social influence: Social norms, conformity, and compliance. In D. T. Gilbert and S. T.Fiske (Eds.), The *Handbook of Social Psychology: Vol. 2.* (4th ed., pp. 151-192). Boston: Mcgraw-Hill.

[vi] Cialdini, R. B., Cacioppo, J. T., Bassett, R., and Miller, J. A. (1978). Low-ball procedure for producing compliance:Commitment then cost. *Journal of Personality and Social Psychology*, 36, 463-476.

viiCialdini, R. B., Cacioppo, J. T., Bassett, R., and Miller, J. A. (1978). Low-ball procedure for producing compliance:Commitment then cost. *Journal of Personality and Social Psychology*, 36, 463-476.

viiiGuéguen N. and Pascual A. (2000), Evocation of freedom and compliance: The "But you arefree of... " technique, *Current Research in Social Psychology*, 5, 264-270.

ix Guadagno, R. E., & Cialdini, R. B. (2002). On-line persuasion: An examination of differences in computer-mediated interpersonal influence. *Group Dynamics: Theory, Research and Practice*, 6, 38–51.

x Cialdini, R. B. (1984). *Influence: The Psychology of Persuasion*. Also published as the textbook

xi Cialdini, R. B. (1984). *Influence: The Psychology of Persuasion*. Also published as the textbook

xii Behm, J. W. (1966). *Theory of psychological reactance.* Academic Press.

lxiiiS. S., & Brehm, J. W. (1981). *Psychological Reactance: A Theory of Freedom and Control.* Academic Press.

xiv Bhm, J. W. (1966). *Theory of Psychological Reactance.* Academic Press.

xv Cialdini, R. B. (1984). *Influence: The Psychology of Persuasion*. Also published as the textbook

xvi Cialdini, R. B. (1984). *Influence: The Psychology of Persuasion*. Also published as the textbook

xviiBehm, J. W. (1966). *Theory of Psychological Reactance.* Academic Press.

xviii Cialdini, R. B. (1984). *Influence: The Psychology of Persuasion*. Also published as the textbook

xix Cialdini, R. B. (1984). *Influence: The Psychology of Persuasion*. Also published as the textbook

xxFehr, Ernst; Simon Gächter (Summer 2000). "Fairness and Retaliation: The Economics of Reciprocity". *Journal of Economic Perspectives*

xxiCialdini, R. B., & Trost, M. R., (1998) Social influence: Social norms, conformity, and compliance. In D. T. Gilbert and S. T.Fiske (Eds.), The *Handbook of Social Psychology: Vol. 2.* (4th ed., pp. 151-192). Boston: Mcgraw-Hill.

xxii Druckman, J.N. (2001). "The Implications of Framing Effects for Citizen Competence". *Political Behavior* **23** (3): 225–256.

xxiii Druckman, J.N. (2001). "The Implications of Framing Effects for Citizen Competence". *Political Behavior* **23** (3): 225–256.

xxiv Abikoff, H; Courtney, M; Pelham, WE; Koplewicz, HS (1993), "Teachers' Ratings of Disruptive Behaviors: TheInfluence of Halo Effects", *Journal of Abnormal Child Psychology* **21** (5): 519–33

xxv Abikoff, H; Courtney, M; Pelham, WE; Koplewicz, HS (1993), "Teachers' Ratings of Disruptive Behaviors: TheInfluence of Halo Effects", *Journal of Abnormal Child Psychology* **21** (5): 519–33

xxvi Cialdini, R. B. (1984). *Influence: The Psychology of Persuasion.* Also published as the textbook

xxvii Cialdini, R. B. (1984). *Influence: The Psychology of Persuasion.* Also published as the textbook

xxviiihttp://www.ncbi.nlm.nih.gov/pubmed/24340812

xxix Druckman, J.N. (2001). "The Implications of Framing Effects for Citizen Competence". *Political Behavior* **23** (3):225–256.

xxx Cialdini, R. B. (1984). *Influence: The Psychology of Persuasion.* Also published as the textbook

xxxi Cialdini, R. B. (1984). *Influence: The Psychology of Persuasion.* Also published as the textbook xxxii Cialdini, R. B. (1984). *Influence: The Psychology of Persuasion*. Also published as the textbook

xxxiiiBales, Robert Freed (1950), *Interaction Process Analysis*, New York: Addison-Wesley. Some studies using the method are included in Hare, A. Paul, Edgar F. Borgatta, & R. F. Bales (1955), *Small Groups: Studies in Social Interaction*, New York

xxxivAronson, E., Wilson, T.D., & Akert, A.M. (2005). *Social Psychology* (5th ed.). Upper Saddle River, NJ: Prentice Hall.

xxxvAronson, E., Wilson, T.D., & Akert, A.M. (2005). *Social Psychology* (5th ed.). Upper Saddle River, NJ: Prentice Hall.

xxxviAronson, E., Wilson, T.D., & Akert, A.M. (2005). *Social Psychology* (5th ed.). Upper Saddle River, NJ: Prentice Hall.

www.ingramcontent.com/pod-product-compliance
Lightning Source LLC
Chambersburg PA
CBHW051219170526
45166CB00005B/1957